The People We Are

By Albert Gardner

Published by Pea Patch Publications
P.O. Box 9163
Chattanooga, TN 37412
Copyright © 2000 Albert Gardner

ISBN: 0615544223
ISBN-13: 978-0615544229

Cover Art Image Credit
J.C. Choate Publications

DEDICATION

To Frances, my best friend, my partner and wife of
forty-four years, who has been with me for "better and
worse", and has always been an asset to me in
preaching the gospel.

Contents

INTRODUCTION

The word Trinity is never used in Scripture to refer to God, but the term Godhead is used to express the fact that there are three Persons yet one God. Though we may not fully understand it, we accept it by faith because the Bible teaches it (Acts 17:29; Colossians 2:9; Daniel 9:25). We should never fall into the trap of thinking there are three Gods. There is one God (Ephesians 4:6), and that one God consists of three Persons, the Father, Son, and Holy Spirit. Each of them, the Father, Son, and Holy Spirit, is called God. Each of them is said to be eternal. Attributes of deity are attributed to all of them. The evidence is great to prove the existence, power, and wisdom of God. The testimony in behalf of Christ as God's Son, is sound and solid as revealed in the gospels. The Holy Spirit is said to be another of the same kind (John 14:16). He is a person just like God and Christ. Those who reject the existence of God have not carefully and honestly examined all the evidence available to them in God's two books: nature and Scripture. A study of the Godhead is one of the most mind stretching subjects possible. God is so great, powerful, and wonderful that we can never learn everything, for "his ways [are] past finding out!" (Romans 11:33). Obviously, this small volume does not begin to exhaust the subject. We have tried to deal with some basic matters regarding the Godhead, with the hope that the reader will have a deeper faith, and that this will stimulate in them a deeper study. It is our prayer that God will be honored and praised.

1 THE GOD WE SERVE - 1

IS THERE A GOD?

In India I saw four men carrying an idol that looked like a lion. I noticed they were carrying the idol and the idol was not carrying them! I wonder if they ever noticed that. It reminded me of the time that Dagon, the Philistine god, fell down when the Ark of the Covenant was placed by it (1 Samuel 5:1-7). He was unable to get up and those who believed in him had to put him back in his place.

A POWER CONTRAST

Idols "Their idols are silver and gold, the work of men's hands. They have mouths, but they speak not: eyes have they, but they see not: they have ears, but they hear not: noses have they, but they smell not: they have hands, but they handle not: feet have they, but they walk not: neither speak they through their throat. They that make them are

1

like unto them; so is every one that trusteth in them" (Psalm 115:4-8).

In Isaiah 44:9-17, a graphic picture is given of those who make idols. They cut down a tree that they did not cause to grow. With part of it they warm themselves and with part of it they cook their food. From the rest of it an idol is carved and people fall down and say "save me."

Idols cannot comfort in sorrow, heal the body in sickness, save the soul in death. The gods depend on those who believe in them and offer no help at all.

The Living God "God that made the world and all things therein, seeing that he is Lord of heaven and earth, dwelleth not in temples made with hands; neither is worshipped with men's hands, as though he needed any thing, seeing he giveth to all life, and breath, and all things; and hath made of one blood all nations of men for to dwell on all the face of the earth, and hath determined the times before appointed, and the bounds of their habitation" (Acts 17:24-26).

The true God is eternal (Psalm 90:2), creates (Genesis 1:1), is all wise (Psalm 139:1-3), all powerful (Genesis 18:14; Matthew 19:26), is present everywhere (Psalm 139:4— 12), guides history (Daniel 2:21; Galatians 4:4; Romans 5:6), forgives sins (Hebrews 8:12), is just (Psalm 89:14), is holy (Isaiah 6:3), and is unchangeable (Malachi 3:6).

THE POWER OF GOD DEMONSTRATED

Creation The Hebrew word for create in Genesis 1:1 is used only of God and is never used of man. He made all things (Acts 14:15).

Israel God promised that He would make a great nation out of Abraham and bless the world through his seed (Genesis 12:1-3; Galatians 3:16-29). At times it looked like Israel would be destroyed but God always preserved them. They went to Egypt and Babylon but God was watching over them so the Savior would be born from the tribe of Judah.

Salvation Only God can save. He has placed the power to save in the gospel, so It becomes evident that where the gospel is not preached, people are not being saved.

Christians Not only does He save sinners but He works in them as Christians. His power works in us (Ephesians 3:20). He can take a drunkard and make a sober person. He can take a liar and make an honest person. He can take a fighter like Saul of Tarsus and make him into the great apostle Paul. He can take a man like Peter who would deny Him and make him into a powerful preacher for Pentecost and have him write two New Testament books. He can clean impure lives and minds and use them for great purposes.

Resurrection God will demonstrate His power on the great resurrection day when the trumpet will sound, Jesus shall appear the second time, and the dead will hear His voice and come forth.

There is a great danger that we will fall into the same trap that Israel did when they "tempted God and limited the Holy One of Israel" (Psalm 78:41).

IS THERE A GOD?

If there is no God, the Bible is a joke, there is no sin, Savior, church, salvation, heaven, hell, or judgment. There is no explanation for the origin of life, the conscience, and the entire world. Everything had been produced by chance and all of it came from lifeless dead matter!

If God really does exist and we are made in His image (Genesis 1:26—27), we know where we came from, what we are to do here, and where we will go when this life is over. We can know our relationship to the physical world and how we are to treat other people. We can be sure there will be a judgment day.

As great as the advantages are if one begins with God, what right do I have to take that view? Must I claim the existence of God without evidence? Must I accept the existence of God blindly? Is there any sound basis for it? Is there sufficient evidence which compels us to believe in God?

> "We are here. The obvious question is this: from whence have we come? There are only two possible explanations. Either life occurred naturally, through some sort of evolutionary process (spontaneous generation via biochemical evolution, etc.), or it occurred supernaturally. These two possibilities

exhaust all the options." ---Douglas Dean, "The Origin of Life", SPIRITUAL SWORD, October 1989, p. 30

The first verse of the Bible begins with God. If one starts with God, the problem of origins is solved. If one rejects God and accepts the natural explanation, there is created some very deep and difficult problems. The natural explanation demands that everything came out of a chaotic and random state by pure chance. This would also mean that matter is eternal and evolved from the lower to the higher forms of life. However, it is pretty much agreed among scientists that matter has not always existed but had a beginning, though there may be disagreement about exactly how or when matter began.

FAITH IS BASED ON EVIDENCE

Believers do not take a leap into the dark; rather they become believers because of available evidence. Unbelievers either do not know the evidence, do not understand the evidence, or they do know and understand it but reject it. Of the Gentiles, Paul wrote, that they did not accept the evidence in nature for the existence of God and that "they are without excuse" (Romans 1:20).

Faith is based on evidence. *"Now is the substance of things hoped for, the evidence of things not seen" (Hebrews 11:1). J. W. McGarvey quotes this verse translated by Edward Robinson. "Faith is confidence as to things hoped for; conviction as to things not seen." Then he adds: "Faith is thus defined as having relation to two classes of objects: things hoped for, and things unseen."* (Sermons, p. 84).

Though one may not have been to London, one has enough evidence that such a place exists. Pictures, radio and television reports, newspaper and magazine articles reveal it. People who have been there confirm it to us. To deny the existence of London is to reject the evidence and means one is unfair and dishonest.

On what basis do we believe in God? No one has seen God, so how can we be sure? We cannot let personal desire determine it for us. Our training and background can be faulty, so there must be greater evidence.

EVIDENCE FOR GOD

"In approaching the study of the arguments used for the existence of God, the following must be borne in mind: (1) that they are not independent proofs of the existence of God, but rather corroborations and expositions of our innate conviction of his existence; (2) that, since God is a spirit, we must not insist on the same type of proof that we demand for the existence of material things, but only on such evidence as is suitable to the object of proof; and (3) that the evidence is cumulative, a single argument for the existence of God being inadequate, but a number of them together being sufficient to bind the conscience and compel belt " ---Henry C. Thiessen, Lectures in Systematic Theology, p 27

The Cosmological Argument This is the idea of an Uncaused First Cause. Every effect has a cause. When we hear a loud noise, someone may ask, "What was that?" It is an accepted fact that something caused the noise.

6

Thiessen stated this argument concisely: "Everything begun must have an adequate cause. The universe was begun; something now exists, (1) something must be eternal unless (2) something comes from nothing." p. 28.

We are here but we didn't cause ourselves. It is clear that we did not just happen because the odds would be too great to think that our complex bodies randomly came out of disorder.

> "The alternative that evolutionists and religious skeptics usually take with respect to the question of a First Cause is to claim that the universe is eternal-- it and our present natural laws have always been in existence." ---3. D. Thomas, FACTS AND FAITH, Vol. I, p 233

The second law of thermodynamics, or entropy, shows that matter had a beginning.

> "It so happens, however, that our present scientific knowledge about the second law of thermodynamics, or entropy establishes rather conclusively that the universe has not always been, but had a beginning, at which time it began the function of radiating or emanating energy, which has been going constantly since that time. It is thus the conclusion of a consensus of scientists that the 'universe is running down' and if this be true, then the assumption that a First Cause is not needed does not stand. Again, science proves favorable to faith." ————Ibid, pp 233—234

The second law of thermodynamics indicates the universe is running down. Energy is becoming less available. When you use a tank of gas in your car, you cannot use it a second time. When a ton of coal is burned, it cannot be burned again. When uranium emits all energy, what is left is lead.

Since matter had a beginning, there must be an adequate intelligent Uncaused Cause to produce it. We believe that Cause to be God.

Teleological Argument This is an argument from design. None can seriously doubt order in the world. Everything produces after its kind. Order prevails with the planets. Gravity works the same way for everyone all the time. All of this shows intelligent design.

> "William Paley (1723-1805) made the argument that a watch requires a watchmaker. The design is so complicated that it would be illogical and unreasonable to believe that the parts of such a timepiece could come together by chance so that the watch would start running and serving its purpose without any planning." ---J.D. Thomas, FACTS AND FAITH, Vol I, p 238

The Bible uses nature as evidence for faith. "The heavens declare the glory of God; and the firmament showeth his handiwork" (Psalm 19:1). "For the invisible things of him from the creation of the world are clearly seen, being understood by the things that are made, even his eternal power and Godhead; so that they are without excuse" (Romans 1:20). "For every house is builded by some man; but he that built all things is God" (Hebrews 3:4).

"Nevertheless he left not himself without witness, in that he did good, and gave us rain from heaven, and fruitful seasons, filling our hearts with food and gladness" (Acts 14:17).

There are many things connected with people and the earth which show signs of intelligence and planning. The animal and vegetable kingdoms are interdependent. The various systems of the body function together in such a way that requires a planner. The solar system works according to law which allows us to know when there will be an eclipse for years ahead. Design implies a designer.

A watch requires a watchmaker. A law demands a law giver. A painting implies an artist. A poem means there is a poet. A world implies a world maker, and we believe the great Designer and Planner to be God.

The Moral Argument This is based on the idea that we do things because of what we think we "ought" to do. Every person has a conscience which hurts when he does something he "ought" not to do.

At a certain age a child comes to the age of accountability w there seems to be'.an of duty and responsibility for what one does. Where did it come from? Long before the Ten Commandments said "Thou shalt not kill", Cain knew he had done wrong and tried to hide it. How did he know that?

Where did the conscience come from? Evolution has no place for the development of the conscience. None of the animals show any signs of remorse or moral consciousness. But human beings have a feeling of ethical responsibility that can only be explained by it being put in him by God.

Ontological Argument   This has to do with the very idea we have of God.   Hoekema says this argument "argues that we have an idea of God.   This idea of God is infinitely greater than man himself.   Hence, it cannot have its origin in man.   It can only have its origin in God Himself." ---Henry C. Thiessen, LECTURES IN SYSTEMATIC THEOLOGY, p. 30

The Bible Argument   We believe in God because we believe the Bible which reveals God.   But one might object that this is reasoning in a circle.   We believe in God because we believe the Bible, and we believe the Bible because we believe in God.   This might be true if there were no evidence for believing the Bible, but the evidence is great which we will discuss in a later chapter.

QUESTIONS

1. Consider the contrast between idols and the Living God.

2. Name and discuss some ways God has demonstrated His power.

3. What are the only two explanations for our existence?

4. Give a current illustration about how faith is based on evidence.

5. Explain the cosmological argument.

6. What does the second law of thermodynamics establish?

7. What is the teleological argument?

8. What was William Paley's illustration of the argument from design?

9. Discuss the moral and ontological arguments.

10. Can we us the Bible to establish the existence of God?

2 THE GOD WE SERVE - 2

What is your view of God?

THE INFIDEL'S CHALLENGE

"If I firmly believed, as millions say they do, that the knowledge and practice of Christianity in this life influences destiny in another world, Christianity would be to me everything! I would cast aside earthly cares and follies, and earthly thoughts and feelings as vanity. Christianity would be my first waking thought and my last image before sleep sank me into unconsciousness. I would labor in its cause alone. I would take thought of the morrow but for eternity alone. Earthly consequences would never stay my hands or seal my lips. I would esteem one soul gained for heaven worth a life time of effort. I would go forth to the world and preach Christ in season and out of season, and my text would be,

'What shall a man profit if he gain the whole world and lose his own soul?'"

In a letter to king Darius, governor Tatnai said he had asked the Jews who commanded them to build the temple and the walls of the city. He also wanted to know their names so he could write them. Their reply was: "We are the servants of the God of heaven and earth, and build the house that was builded these many years ago, which a great king of Israel builded and set up" (Ezra 5:11).

Jehovah is not a national God like Dagon was for the Philistines, but is "God of heaven and earth." There is a sense in which He is referred to as the "God of Israel."

Ezra "was a ready scribe in the law of Moses which the Lord God of Israel had given: and the king granted him all his request according to the hand of the Lord his God upon him" (Ezra 7:6). This verse not only shows that He is the God of Israel but that He is Ezra's personal God.

Our God is universal yet He is interested in every individual. The apostle John said the Lamb was "worthy to take the book and open the seals thereof: for thou wast slain, and hast redeemed us to God by thy blood out of every kindred, and tongue, and people, and nation" (Revelation 5:9). For this reason the word of God is not bound to a certain land, people, language, or method of teaching. "For God is the King of all the earth" (Psalm 47:7).

Satan's View Satan convinced Eve that God was withholding good things from her and that is the reason she was told not to eat of the fruit. He said, "For God doth know that in the day ye eat thereof, then your eyes shall be opened, and ye shall be a gods, knowing good and evil" (Genesis 3:5).

After Adam and Eve ate of the forbidden fruit, their eyes were opened alright, for they could see themselves in sin, their separation from God, and some of the immediate consequences of their disobedience. They could also see that God is truthful and that He did exactly what He told them would happen.

God made us and knows what is good for us and instructs us in ways that will bring happiness in this life and will bring us to heaven. Sometimes children get the idea that their parents will not permit them to engage in many things because they don't want them to enjoy the good life. The true situation is that these parents are not permissive because they know the dangers and pit-falls which would destroy the good life. These parents know more than their children, just as our heavenly Father knows what is good for us. The limits God has given are for our happiness and well being (Psalm 84:11).

Solomon was not to marry foreign women because they would bring their idolatry with them and they would turn away his heart after their gods. God knew more about Solomon than Solomon knew about himself for it happened just as God had told him. "For it came to pass, when Solomon was old, that his wives turned away his heart after other gods: and his heart was not perfect with the Lord his God, as was the heart of David his father" (1 Kings 11:4). Since the restrictions were given for Solomon's good, to reject these restrictions was not just unwise, but is called sin (Nehemiah 13:26).

Cain's View Like many today, Cain thought he could substitute in worship to God, which really strikes at the authority of God. The rejection of Cain and his sacrifice led him to kill his brother and try to hid his dark deed from God. But God asked him: "What hast thou done? The voice of thy brother's blood crieth unto me from the ground" (Genesis 4:10). God is ever present and nothing is hid from Him. "All things are naked and opened unto the eyes of him with whom we have to do" (Hebrews 4:13).

Pharaoh's View What we think of God determines what we will do, how we will treat others, and in fact, it determines our relationship to everything. Moses and Aaron went to Pharaoh and told him God said "let my people go, that they may hold a feast unto me in the wilderness. And Pharaoh said, Who is the Lord, that I should obey his voice to let Israel go? I know not the Lord, neither will I let Israel go" (Exodus 5:1-2).

What a difference it would have made had he known and believed God! His actions were set by what he believed about God just as ours are today.

Why is one fair in his dealing, clean in his speech, and sincere in his worship? Isn't it because he believes there is a God to whom he is responsible and accountable? Don't we strive to be like Him who is fair and true in every respect? Were it not for this view and influence, everyone would be a law unto himself and it would not really be safe for any of us.

Syrian View Because the Syrians lost in their battle with Israel, they said: "the Lord is God of the hills, but he is not God of the valleys" (1 Kings 20:28). What a senseless view of God, which limited His power and presence. It is so easy to fall into that trap in our own lives. We know God is so powerful that He made the world but we think He may not be able to help us solve our daily problems. If we could always live on the plains, He would always be there to help, but He is not a God of the valleys.

God vs Baal Ahab asked Elijah, "Art thou he that troubleth Israel?" Elijah replied that the trouble was caused by Israel under his leadership in that they had forsaken the commandments of the Lord and had followed Baal. He challenged the 450 prophets of Baal to prove who is God by offering a sacrifice to see who would answer by fire. He stated the choices. "If the Lord be God, follow him: but if Baal, then follow him."

At the suggestion of Elijah, the prophets of Baal went first for they were many. They prepared a bullock by cutting it in pieces and laying it on the wood but put no fire under it. The prophets of Baal cried from morning till noon to Baal but there was no voice or answer. Elijah mocked them by saying he may be talking, taking a journey, or he might be asleep. Baal had failed them.

After midday, Elijah took twelve stones according to the twelve tribes and built an altar. He cut the bullock in pieces and laid him on the altar. After he had made a trench around the altar he poured four barrels of water on the sacrifices and the wood. He did this three times which saturated the sacrifices and filled the trench with water.

This great prophet of God uttered a simple but powerful prayer. "Lord God of Abraham, Isaac, and of Israel, let it be known this day that thou art God in Israel, and that I am thy servant, and that I have done, all these things at thy word. Hear me, 0 Lord, hear me, that this people may know that thou art the Lord God, and that thou hast turned their heart back again" (1 Kings 18:36-37).

The answer was clear and the result was final. "Then the fire of the Lord fell, and consumed the burnt sacrifice, and the wood, and the stones, and the dust, and licked up the water that was in the trench. And when all the people saw it, they fell on their faces: and they said, The Lord, he is the God; and the Lord, he is the God" (1 Kings 18:38-39).

Paul's view All who study the life of the apostle Paul will admit he was honest and sincere, even when he was wrong. He was that way before he became a Christian, so that part he did not have to change. His faith in God was deep. His actions were based on the view that God loved him, saved him, providentially guided him, and had a work for him to do that was important. Because of this view he was willing to spend and be spent in the cause of our Lord. He was not only willing to suffer, he was ready to die for it.

Here are some verses that reveal Paul's view of God. (2 Timothy 1:12; Ephesians 3:20; Philippians 4:13, 19; Romans 8:28; 1 Corinthians 10:13; Galatians 2:20; 2 Timothy 4:7—8; 2 Corinthians 9:8, 15; 3:3).

What Is Your View? It is important that we have the right view of God, for this will determine what we do, think, and say. What we think of God determines:

1. what we do with the commands of God.
2. how we treat others.

18

3. our worship: content, manner, object, or even whether we worship.
4. our view of the Bible.
5. our view of the origin of the world.
6. our view of sin, salvation, the church, a Saviour.
7. our view of life.
8. our view of heaven and hell.
9. our values.

QUESTIONS

1. Discuss how God is used in Ezra 5:11; 7:6 and Psalm 47:7.

2. Discuss Satan's view of God.

3. Discuss Cain's view of God.

4. How did the Pharaoh's view of God affect what he did to Israel?

5. What was the Syrian view of God?

6. Discuss the contest between God and Baal.

7. Discuss some verses in which Paul reveals his view of God.

8. Make application as to how our view of God determines what we do.

ALBERT GARDNER

3 THE CHRIST WE HONOR - 1

Who is Jesus?

The nature of Christ has been a topic of controversy even before His conception. Mary asked, "How can this be, seeing I know not a man?" The angel Gabriel answers her question. "The Holy Ghost shall come upon thee, and the power of the Highest shall overshadow thee: therefore also that holy thing which shall be born of thee shall be called the Son of God" (Luke 1:35).

The whole issue of the credibility of Christianity turns on the nature and sonship of Jesus Christ. If there is no proof for His claims, people could not be held guilty and condemned for their unbelief. If His claims are true, none can be saved without a full acceptance of Him and His teaching.

Who is Jesus?

This question arose often during the life of our Lord which is some indication of its importance. Jesus asked the apostles what people were saying about Him. Some thought He was John, Elijah, Jeremiah, or one of the prophets. Then He asked them, "But whom say ye that I am?"

It makes a difference for it has to do with the foundation of the church. Peter said, "Thou are the Christ, the Son of the living God." On this rock, Jesus promised to build His church (Matthew 16:13-18).

Jesus raised the question again in Matthew 22:41-46, by asking "What think ye of Christ? whose son is he?" They replied, "David." Of course, He was of the lineage of David but He was also David's Lord. He existed before David though He was David's son.

When the Lord appeared to Saul on the Damascus road, Saul asked, "Who art thou, Lord?" It makes all the difference as to whether we must hear or not.

On the mount of transfiguration, the heavenly Father identified Jesus by saying, "This is my beloved Son in whom I am well pleased, hear ye him" (Matthew 17:5).

ARE THE WITNESSES RELIABLE

We believe in Christ because of what is written about Him in the Bible (John 20:30-31). But can we depend on what they wrote? Did they tell the truth? Are they credible? In a court of law, if a witness can be discredited, his testimony will be of little value. Can we accept the testimony of the witnesses concerning Christ? Since faith is based on testimony, we need to know if the witnesses were truthful.

McClintock and Strong, Vol viii, p. 1056, give the following reasons for the reliability of the witnesses of Christ in the New Testament.

1. The nature of these witnesses. They were poor.

2. The number of the witnesses. There was no collusion.

3. The facts which they avowed by the senses (1 John 1:1-4).

4. The agreement of the witnesses.

5. Observe the tribunals before which they gave evidence.

6. The place in which they bore their testimony.

7. The time of this testimony.

8. The motives which induced them to publish the resurrection.

J.W. McGarvey, in Evidences of Christianity, Part 2, page 146, says the "force of human testimony depends on three things." He names: honesty of the witnesses, their competency, and their number.

The Bible writers are credible, so their testimony is reliable. Since the evidence is overwhelming, we turn now to examine some of it.

EVIDENCE JESUS CHRIST AS THE SON OF GOD

"At the mouth of two witnesses, or three witnesses, shall he that is worthy of death be put to death; but at the mouth of one witness he shall not be put to death" (Deuteronomy 17:6). Jesus used that Old Testament principle to prove who He was in the eyes of the people.

"And yet if I judge, my judgment is true: for I am not alone, but I and the Father that sent me. It is also written in your law, that the testimony of two or three men is true. I am one that bear witness of myself, and the Father that sent me beareth witness of me" (John 8:16-18).

He uses this same concept in John 5:31. "If I bear witness of myself, my witness is not true." If He is the only witness, according to Deuteronomy 17:6, He is not to be accepted. Then, He proceeds to offer other witnesses.

John the Baptist "There is another that beareth witness of me; and I know that the witness which he witnesseth is true. Ye sent unto John, and he bare witness unto the truth" (John 5:32-33).

John was asked if he were the Christ, or Elijah, or that Prophet. He answered, "I am not." He said the one who sent him to baptize told him that when he saw the Spirit descend and remain that, he would know that this was the Christ. When he baptized Jesus in the Jordan, he saw that happen. "And I saw, and bare record that this is the Son of God" (John 1:34).

Using the principle that "every word being established by two or three witnesses", His identity is proved, since there are two witnesses: Christ and John.

Works "But I have greater witness than that of John: for the works which the Father hath given me to finish, the same works that I do, bear witness of me, that the Father hath sent me" (John 5:36).

Nicodemus said, "We know thou art a teacher come form God: for no man can do these miracles that thou doest, except God be with him" (John 3:2).

After John was put in prison, he sent two disciples to ask Him if He is the one that should come or should they look for another. Jesus told them to tell John what they hear and see. "The blind receive their sight, and the lame walk, the lepers are cleansed, and the deaf hear, the dead are raised up, and the poor have the gospel preached to them" (Matthew 11:5).

It is by the miracles of Christ that God showed His approval of Jesus (Acts 2:22). The works of Christ tell us that He is the Son of God.

Father "And the Father himself, which hath sent me, hath borne witness of me" (John 5:37). On two public occasions (at His baptism and transfiguration), the Father said, "This is my beloved Son in whom I am well pleased" (Matthew 3:17; 17:5).

There are more than two or three witnesses. So far, we have seen the testimony of Christ, John, His works, and the testimony of the Father. This is convincing evidence.

Scriptures "Search the scriptures; for in them ye think ye have eternal life: and they are they which testify of me" (John 5:39). There are some three hundred prophecies, promises, and types of Christ in the Old Testament, and He fulfilled them all. The evidence is mounting.

Fulfilled prophecy is one of the strongest arguments for the inspiration of the Bible and the deity of Christ. Micah 5:2 stated that Jesus would be born in Bethlehem. Psalm 22:16-18 says His hands and feet would be pierced (John 20:25); that His bones would not be broken (John 19:36); and they would cast lots for His garments (John 19:24).

Resurrection The climax to Peter's Pentecost sermon was the resurrection of Christ and His ascension to the right hand of God. On the third day the tomb was empty, an accepted fact by both friend and foe. Through the centuries the empty tomb has affirmed the deity of Jesus Christ.

Peter's sermon was so convincing that about three thousand gladly received his word and were baptized. They believed what Peter preached about David and Christ David had foretold a time when one would die but his body would not see corruption (Acts 2:27). Peter said David could not have been writing about himself because he died and is still in the grave, which means his body did see corruption.

"Therefore being a prophet, and knowing that God had sworn with an oath to him, that of the fruit of his loins, according to the flesh, he would raise up Christ to sit on his throne; he seeing this before spake of the resurrection of

Christ, that his soul was not left in hell, neither his flesh did see corruption" (Acts 2:30-31.

Mary the Mother Jesus   One charge against Jesus before He went to the cross was "he made himself the Son of God" (John 19:7).   Among those around the cross was Mary and she never said a word.

She knew who His Father was but her silent testimony speaks loud and clear. If Jesus were not the Son of God, she could have told them who His Father really was but she said nothing and let the claim stand. It would be hard to imagine a mother doing nothing if she had the power to stop the suffering and death of her son and would not do it. By her silent testimony we see this as evidence that Jesus is the Son of God.

His Life and Example   No one ever lived like Jesus. He is the only one ever to keep the law perfectly. He always said and did the right things. His motives and desires were spotless. His attitude toward people and things was flawless. His love for every person in the world was genuine. When He was abused, He did not retaliate. He was always interested in the salvation of sinners. None could accuse Him of sin and make it stick (John 8:46).

The evidence for Jesus as the Christ is overwhelming. We have seen many witnesses: John, His works, Father, scriptures, resurrection, silent testimony of Mary, and the perfect example of Christ.

<u>ARIUS</u>

In an address Alexander was insisting that "the Son is co-eternal, co-essential, and co-equal with the Father". Anus opposed him and "asserted that there was a time when the Son was not, since the Father who begot must be before the Son who was begotten, and the latter, therefore, could not be eternal." This account by early writers tells of the origin of this controversy.

--CYCLOPEDIA OF BIBLICAL, THEOLOGICAL, AND ECCLESIASTICAL LITERATURE, McClintock-Strong, Vol I, p 388

The Council of Nice, in 325, was called by Constantine to settle the controversy about the nature of Christ. In our day, the Jehovah's Witnesses teach the view of Christ that Anus taught. We need to examine the Bible, for it reveals the truth, regardless what the councils of men may teach.

Jesus is called the Son of God (Luke 1:35). The Father said, "This is my beloved Son" (Matthew 17:5). However, before Jesus came into the world He is called the Son only in prospect or prophecy.

> "The Scripture nowhere calls Jesus Christ the eternal Son of God, and He is never called Son at all prior to the incarnation, except in prophetic passages in the Old Testament."

> ---Walter Martin, THE KINGDOM OF THE CULTS, P 117

God is eternal but He is not called the "eternal Father", just as Jesus is not called the "eternal Son." Only the Holy Spirit is called the "eternal Spirit" (Hebrews 9:14). The Father--Son relationship did not begin until the conception and birth of Christ.

> "I use the names Father and Son proleptically, or by anticipation, just as we speak of Abraham before he left Ur of Chaldea, though he was not called Abraham for twenty-nine years afterward. In like manner the Messiah is called Son in the second Psalm; though Gabriel said to Mary, "that holy thing that shall be born of thee shall be called the Son of God" (Luke 1:35).
>
> ---Robert Milligan, THE SCHEME OF REDEMPTION, pp 222-223

Conclusion

The evidence is overwhelming in favor of Jesus Christ as the Son of God. His claims are valid, His promises true, and His commands are to be obeyed. Everyone should bow their knee before the King of kings in humble obedience, so when He bursts through the clouds where every eye shall see Him, and the trumpet shall sound and the dead shall arise, we will be able to hear His welcome voice say "well done, thou good and faithful servant." By His grace we will be permitted to go to the place where "God shall wipe away all tears from their eyes; and there shall be no more death, neither sorrow, nor crying, neither shall there be any more pain: for the former things are passed away" (Revelation 21:4).

<u>Questions</u>

1. Discuss how the credibility of Christianity turns on the Sonship of Jesus Christ.

2. Notice verses where the question is raised as to who Jesus is.

3. Since we must depend on the Bible writers for evidence, how may we know if these writers are credible?

4. Discuss one by one, seven witnesses to the deity of Christ.

5. What was the claim of Anus about Christ?

6. Explain when Jesus became a "Son", an how He is called "Son" in the Old Testament.

4 THE CHRIST WE HONOR - 2

He is God

What one thinks of the nature of Christ will determine how one treats the claims and commands of Christ. If He is just a human being like we are, or has been created like other things, we would not feel duty bound to follow Him. A search of the Scriptures will reveal His true nature.

He is God

Hebrews 1:8 "But unto the Son he saith, Thy throne, 0 God, is for ever and ever: a sceptre of righteousness is the sceptre of thy kingdom." This is a quotation of Psalm 45:6-7 and is applied to Christ. The Son is called God. He is not God the Father or God the Holy Spirit but is God the Son.

Matthew 1:23 "Behold, a virgin shall be with child, and shall bring forth a son, and they shall call his name Immanuel, which being interpreted is, God with us." It says God is with us, but of course, Jesus is the one who was with us.

John 1:1 "In the beginning was the Word, and the Word was with God, and the Word was God." Jesus is here called the Word. Verse 14 says "the Word was made flesh, and dwelt among us." Paul says "God was manifest in the flesh" (1 Timothy 3:16).

John 17:5 "And now, 0 Father, glorify thou me with thine own self with the glory which I had with thee before the world was." Jesus was not created and did not begin to have an existence when He was born but was in eternity with God where He was equal with God (Philippians 2:6).

THINGS ASCRIBED TO CHRIST SHOW DEITY

Create Anyone who believes the Bible understands that "In the beginning God created the heaven and the earth" (Genesis 1:1). John saw God on the throne and said, "Thou art worthy, 0 Lord, to receive glory and honor and power: for thou hast created all things, and for thy pleasure they are and were created" (Revelation 4:11). "Before the mountains were brought forth, or ever thou hadst formed the earth and the world, even from everlasting to everlasting, thou art God" (Psalm 90:2). Passages could be multiplied that teach God created the world.

God created but Jesus is the agent of creation. God created the world by Him. Of Christ it is said, "All things were made by him; and without him was not any thing made that was made" (John 1:3). "By whom also he made the worlds" (Hebrews 1:2). "And to make all men see what is the fellowship of the mystery, which from the beginning of the world hath been hid in God, who created all things by Jesus Christ" (Ephesians 3:9).

Only God can create. But Jesus created. Therefore, Jesus is God.

Worship In Matthew 4:10 Jesus quoted Deuteronomy 6:13, when Satan asked Jesus to worship him. "Thou shalt worship the Lord thy God, and him only shalt thou serve."

We must not worship men for Cornelius tried that (Acts 10:25-26). We must not worship angels for John tried that (Revelation 19:10). Jesus said only God is to worshipped.

It is evident that Jesus did receive worship and did not rebuke those who offered it. The blind man believed and worshipped Him (John 9:38). A leper worshipped Him (Matthew 8:2). A woman from Canaan worshipped Him and asked for help (Matthew 15:25).

Hebrews 1:6 is a quotation of Psalm 97:7. "And let all the angels of God worship him." The application of this verse is that even the angels are to worship Him, thus showing that He is God, for God only is to be worshipped. Only of God can it be said that "every knee should bow" but Paul says this of Christ (Philippians 2:10).

Only God is to be worshipped. Jesus accepted worship. Therefore, Jesus is God.

Forgiveness Jesus told the palsied man his sins were forgiven, and the scribes were right when they asked "who can forgive sins but God only?" No man can forgive sins, yet Jesus did it. The scribes were wrong in thinking Jesus was only a man.

There is a sense in which one person can forgive another after we sin against them, but in the absolute sense, only God can forgive (Ephesians 4:32).

Only God can forgive. Jesus did forgive sins. Therefore, Jesus is God.

CHRIST IS THE CREATOR OF ALL THINGS

Colossians 1:15-17 The New World Translation, published by Watchtower Bible and Tract Society, is the Bible used by Jehovah's Witnesses. It is unacceptable because it was translated in ways to teach their doctrines. Notice how additions are made to Colossians 1:15-17. "He is the image of the invisible God, the first-born of all creation; because by means of him all [other] things were created in the heavens and upon the earth, the things visible and the things invisible, no matter whether they are thrones of lordships or governments or authorities. All [other] things have been created through him and for him. Also, he is before all [other] things and by means of him all [other] things were made to exist."

They add in brackets the word "other" and there is absolutely no justification for it. Consider the same passage from a correct translation. "Who is the image of the invisible God, the firstborn of every creature: for by him were all things created, that are in heaven, and that are in earth, visible and invisible, whether they be thrones, or dominions, or principalities, or powers: all things were created by him, and for him: and he is before all things, and by him all things consist."

From this we learn that He is the creator of all things. He is not a part of the "things" created. He was before them. Everything that was created was created by Him. "All things were made by him; and without him was not any thing made that was made" (John 1:3).

Firstborn Another attempt to get the Bible to teach that Jesus was created is based on Revelation 3:14. "These things saith the Amen, the faithful and true witness, the beginning of the creation of God." Also, Colossians 1:15. "Who is the image of the invisible God, the firstborn of every creature."

In the Old Testament the firstborn was to inherit a double portion (Deuteronomy 21:16-17). Jesus was the firstborn son of Mary (Luke 2:7), because other children would follow. In point of time He was first, but Jesus was not the first thing created for He was "before all things", so was not created at all. Because he was the beginner and author of all creation, He was the firstborn of creation as a place of honor, like the firstborn in a Jewish family. He is "the beginning of the creation of God." He is not the beginning in the sense of the first thing created, but He is the beginning of the creation in the sense of being the beginner of the creation of all things.

Proverbs 8:22 "The Lord possessed me in the beginning of his way, before his works of old." "The Lord produced me" (NWT). It is claimed that God produced Jesus before His works of old and that Jesus then, created all [other] things.

This verse does not refer to Christ but to wisdom. The context from verse one of this chapter is talking about wisdom. It is by wisdom God created the world, princes rule, and riches are brought forth. By reading the chapter we know it is talking about wisdom, so one would never think to apply verse 22 to Christ.

TRINITY

The word trinity does not appear in the Bible but the idea is there. Do not make the mistake of thinking there are three Gods. There is one God (Ephesians 4:6). "Hear, 0 Israel: the Lord our God is one Lord" (Deuteronomy 6:4). "Remember the former things of old: for I am God, and there is none else; I am God, and there is none like me" (Isaiah 46:9).

That there are three members of the Godhead is taught in at least three ways in the Bible.

Words Which Imply More Than One "Let us make man" (Genesis 1:26). Though that may not tell us there are three, "us" does mean there is more than one. "In the beginning was the Word, and the Word was with God, and the Word was God" (John 1:1). Jesus was "with" God, which means there were at least two. So does the word "both" in 2 John 9.

In John 14:16, Jesus promised the Holy Spirit to the apostles. "And I will pray the Father, and he shall give you another Comforter, that he may abide with you for ever." The Greek word translated "another", means another of the same kind. One could have an apple in one hand and an orange in the other hand. That would be another but not of the same kind. If one has an apple in one hand and an apple in the other hand, it would be another of the same kind. Jesus promised "another of the same kind." The Holy Spirit was another like Jesus the Son and God the Father.

Verses Which Include The Three When Jesus was baptized in the Jordan by John we can see all three persons in the Godhead (Matthew 3:13-17). Jesus was standing in the water, the Father's voice was heard from heaven, and the Holy Spirit descended like a dove.

In the Great Commission, Jesus told the apostles to go and "teach all nations, baptizing them in the name of the Father, and of the Son, and of the Holy Ghost" (Matthew 28:19).

"But when the Comforter is come, whom I will send unto you from the Father, even the Spirit of truth, which proceedeth from the Father, he shall testify of me" (John 15:26).

"How much more shall the blood of Christ, who through the eternal Spirit offered himself without spot to God, purge your conscience from dead works to serve the living God?" (Hebrews 9:14).

Each Is Called God "Peace be to the brethren, and love with faith, from God the Father and the Lord Jesus Christ" (Ephesians 6:23).

Many passages show Jesus is God. In Matthew 1:23, He is "God with us." Hebrews 1:8 is a quotation of Psalm 45:6-7. The writer of Hebrews applies it to Christ. "But unto the Son he saith, Thy throne 0 God, is for ever and ever: a sceptre of righteousness is the sceptre of thy kingdom." The meaning is clear. In the Old Testament God the Father called Jesus God.

When Ananias and Sapphira sold their land, they kept back some of the price and claimed this was the full price they were giving. "But Peter said, Ananias, why hath Satan filled thine heart to lie to the Holy Ghost, and to keep back part of the price of the land? While it remained, was it not thine own? And after it was sold, was it not in thine own power? why hast thou conceived this thing in thine heart? thou hast not lied unto men, but unto God (Acts 5:3-4). He had lied to the Holy Spirit but Peter said he had lied to God. The Holy Spirit is God. He is not God the Son but God the Holy Spirit.

How is it possible to have three in the Godhead and there be only one God? Several attempts have been made to explain it, though none of them may completely satisfy.

A table, a door, and a desk are three but they are one in that all of them are made from wood. Ice, snow, and rain are three yet they are one in that they are water. In the same way, the Father, Son, and Holy Spirit are different Persons but they are one in nature and in their purposes for us.

How are husband and wife one? Are they one person? They are not, but the Bible says they are one (Matthew 19:6). Even Christians are to be one. Jesus prayed that we might be one as He and His Father are one (John 17:20-21).

Though we may not fully explain or understand how there can be three Persons, yet one God, we can nevertheless believe it. It is not necessary to understand something before we accept it, for we do not fully understand gravity, electricity, or how a seed can produce another plant, but we fully accept all of these. We must be united that there is one God who is all-wise, all-powerful, and self-existent.

The Bible reveals God but with our finite minds we are unable to understand the infinite. That does not mean we cannot understand anything, for nature and revelation both tell us something about God. From nature we can learn about the existence and power of God (Romans 1:20; Psalm 19:1). Without Scripture to tell us about the nature, love, and holiness of God, we would turn to the worship of the sun, moon, and stars or other things of creation. But even with Scripture we cannot fully comprehend God. "O the depth of the riches both of the wisdom and knowledge of God! how unsearchable are his judgments, and his ways past finding out!" (Romans 11:33).

QUESTIONS

1. Discuss verses which teach Jesus is God.

2. Name and discuss three things ascribed to Jesus which show He is deity.

3. Discuss Colossians 1:15-17 and related verses, which declare that Jesus is the creator and not a part of that which was created.

4. How is the firstborn used in the Bible?

5. What is the context of Proverbs 8:22?

6. Name and discuss three ways we may conclude the Bible teaches the trinity.

5 THE CHRIST WE HONOR - 3

Ways We Honor Christ

In Revelation 5, the apostle John wept because no one was found in heaven or earth worthy to open the book and break the seals. The angel told John not to weep because the Lion of the tribe of Judah would open the book. When John looked, instead of a Lion, he saw a Lamb that had been slain. He heard the voice of tens of thousands of angels say, "Worthy is the Lamb that was slain to receive power, and riches, and wisdom, and strength, and honor, and glory, and blessing" (Revelation 5:12).

Tillit S. Teddlie wrote the beautiful song "Worthy Art Thou", based on this passage.

Worthy of praise is Christ our Redeemer,
Worthy of glory honor and power!
Worthy of all our soul's adoration,
Worthy art Thou! Worthy art Thou!

Jesus deserves honor because of who He is. He is God. He is the Son of God. He is the Lion with power, but He is the Lamb who meekly died for us.

Jesus deserves honor because of what He has done for us. "Who gave himself for our sins, that he might deliver us from this present evil world, according to the will of God and our Father" (Galatians 1:4). Without Him there is no hope. He is the way, the truth, and the life. He is our sacrifice, mediator, high priest, and king.

Jesus deserves honor because of where he has gone. When He ascended back to heaven, He sat down on the right hand of God. In the prayer before the cross, He asked for His former glory.

"I have glorified thee on the earth: I have finished the work which thou gayest me to do. And now, O Father, glorify thou me with thine own self with the glory which I had with thee before the world was" (John 17:4-5).

Often those who believe Christ should be honored, and even desire to do so, fail because they do not know what is required to give honor to Him. They misunderstand the ways we honor Him. We honor a judge by standing when he enters. Children are to told to "honor thy father and mother." How do children do that? There may be several ways we honor our parents, but one way is to obey them.

There are many definite ways we honor Christ, which we can know and observe. Without a knowledge of these ways, we might be trying to honor Him in ways which would actually be dishonoring Him.

WE HONOR HIM BY TEACHING HIS WORD

It is not possible to separate Christ and His word. "He that rejecteth me, and receiveth not my words, hath one that judgeth him: the word that I have spoken, the same shall judge him in the last day" (John 12:48).

It is dishonor to Christ if we fail to teach His word, or if we teach something different from His word. To abide in the doctrine of Christ is so important, for without it we do not have God (2 John 9). The wrong teaching will make vain worship (Matthew 15:9).

One cannot be taught wrong and baptized right. Wrong teaching makes wrong worship. If we give careful attention to teaching the doctrine of Christ, we are respecting His authority.

WE HONOR CHRIST IN BAPTISM

Our baptism is into the death of Christ, where He poured out His blood for our sins. We obey the form of doctrine, which is the death, burial, and resurrection of Christ. We die to the practice of sin by repentance. We are buried in baptism, like He was buried, and we are raised like He was raised (Romans 6:3-5). By doing this we express our faith in His death, burial, and resurrection.

Baptism is in the name of Christ (Acts 2:38; 19:1—7) which means it is by His authority. He is the one who commanded it, and we do it in the name of the Father, Son, and Holy Spirit (Matthew 28:19). When people are baptized in the name of the Father, Son, and Holy Spirit, they honor Christ by obeying Him. To refuse baptism is to dishonor Him for we have rejected His authority.

WE HONOR HIS DEATH IN THE LORD'S SUPPER

Death is not usually considered good news, but the death of Christ is good news because He "died for our sins" (1 Corinthians 15:3).

When Jesus gave the Lord's Supper, He said, "For this is the blood of the new testament, which is shed for many for the remission of sins" (Matthew 26:28). As we study the Bible and make a clear distinction between the Old and New Testaments, we honor what His death on the cross accomplished (Colossians 2:14). Binding Old Testament law today dishonors Christ, by denying the power of the cross.

As we eat the bread and drink the fruit of the vine, we focus our thinking on His body and blood. "For as often as ye eat this bread, and drink this cup, ye do show the Lord's death till he come" (1 Corinthians 11:26). We are not remembering His birth or His resurrection, but His death. Each first day of the week, we do this in remembrance of His death.

To neglect to eat the Lord's Supper each Lord's Day is to dishonor Christ and His death, by failing to do what He asked us to do. This duty and privilege should never be taken lightly, for those who fail to do it become spiritually weak, sickly, and sleepy (1 Corinthians 11:30).

WE HONOR HIS RESSURECTION ON THE LORD'S DAY

The Sabbath ended at the cross, and its observance was never commanded of Christians. Psalm 118:22-24 teaches that the Lord's Day is the day Jesus was made the head stone of the corner. He became the head stone of the corner when He was raised from the dead. He was raised from the dead on the first day of the week. So, the Lord's Day is the first day of the week.

The first day is the Lord's Day because He was raised that day. We worship on the first day of the week and honor His resurrection. We are to give of our money on that day (1 Corinthians 16:2). The Lord's Supper is to be eaten on the first day of the week (Acts 20:7). The apostle John said he was in the Spirit on the Lord's Day (Revelation 1:10). Every Christian should assemble with fellow Christians to worship and honor Him on His day.

WE HONOR CHRIST IN HIS CHURCH

In the Old Testament, Israel was married to God (Jeremiah 3:14), and in the New Testament we are married to Christ (Romans 7:4). The church is the bride of Christ, and as such, she wears His name, honors His authority, and obeys His will. Individual Christians should do nothing that will bring dishonor and shame on the bride.

It is of no value to talk about being saved outside the church, for the divinely designated place of glory and honor is the church. "Unto him be glory in the church by Christ Jesus throughout all ages, world without end" (Ephesians 3:21).

Some who think Christ should be honored, and are trying to do so, neglect to see that one way we honor Him is by being in His church and leading others to faithfulness in His church.

WE HONOR HIM BY CHRISTIAN LIVING

Example It is so harmful to the cause of Christ when members of the church don't live right. In the Christians armor, we are to have our "loins girt about with truth", but are also to have on the "breastplate of righteousness" (Ephesians 6: 14). Truth will not move people to obey unless it is coupled with right living.

Our Lord taught that if we live right before others, they will glorify God because of our example.

"Let your light so shine before men, that they may see your good works, and glorify your Father which is in heaven" (Matthew 5:16).

"Having your conversation honest among the Gentiles: that, whereas they speak against you as evildoers, they may by your good works, which they shall behold, glorify God in the day of visitation" (1 Peter 2:12).

Christian Families Some of the greatest work in all the world, is done by mothers and fathers who love, train, and discipline their children, so they grow up to be faithful Christians. Weak teaching and poor examples before the children, usually does not train them to put the church or spiritual matters first in their lives.

One generation without God is caused by neglecting to teach the children (Psalm 78:4-8; Judges 2:10).

46

Worships One basic idea in worship is honor. The power, love, and majesty of God demands honor. "Thou shalt worship the Lord thy God, and him only shalt thou serve" (Matthew 4:10).

Our worship honors Him only if we honor His authority and offer only prescribed worship in the way He said do it (John 4:24). "And whatsoever ye do in word or deed, do all in the name of the Lord Jesus, giving thanks to God and the Father by him" (Colossians 3:17).

When we consider God and what He has done for us, along with David we should ask, "What is man, that thou art mindful of him? and the son of man, that thou visitest him?" (Psalm 8:4).

QUESTIONS

1. Consider Revelation 5 and the importance of honoring Christ.

2. Discuss reasons why Jesus deserves honor.

3. Discuss one by one, ways we may honor Christ.

4. Show how one can be religious and sincerely desire to honor Christ, but it would actually be dishonor.

ALBERT GARDNER

6 THE SPIRIT WE HAVE

The Holy Spirit is the third member of the Godhead. He is a person, not a feeling or some impersonal force. Jehovah's Witnesses translation calls the Spirit "God's active force" (Genesis 1:2 NWT).

The Holy Spirit is God. When Ananias brought the price of his land and kept back part of it, "Peter said, Ananias, why hath Satan filled thine heart to lie to the Holy Ghost, and to keep back part of the price of the land?" (Acts 5:3). In verse four he is told "thou has not lied unto men, but unto God." This shows that the Holy Spirit is God. He is not God the Father, and He is not God the Son, but He is God the Holy Spirit.

In 2 Timothy 3:16 we are told that "all Scripture is given by inspiration of God." God inspired the Scriptures. However, in 1 Corinthians 2:11-13 we learn that the Holy Spirit is the one who inspired the Bible writers. The mystery was "revealed unto his holy apostles and prophets by the Spirit" (Ephesians 3:5).

DEITY DWELLS IN CHRISTIANS

God Dwells in Us "And what agreement hath the temple of God with idols? for ye are the temple of the living God; as God hath said, I will dwell in them, and walk in them; and I will be their God, and they shall be my people" (2 Corinthians 6:16)

Christs Dwells in Us "Which is Christ in you, the hope of glory" (Colossians 1:27).

Holy Spirit Dwells in Us "But ye are not in the flesh, but in the Spirit, if so be that the Spirit of God dwell in you. Now if any man have not the Spirit of Christ, he is none of his" (Romans 8:9). "What! know ye not that your body is the temple of the Holy Ghost which is in you, which ye have of God, and ye are not your own?" (1 Corinthians 6:19). "Know ye not that ye are the temple of God, and that the Spirit of God dwelleth in you?" (1 Corinthians 3:16).

HOW THE HOLY SPIRIT DWELLS IN CHRISTIANS

Whether the Holy Spirit dwells in Christians has never been the issue with Bible believing people, for the word of God is very clear on this point. There are two views. 1) There is the personal indwelling of the Spirit, and

2) The Spirit dwells in us through the word He has given. Leading brethren have taken both views. Before we study this further, we should notice these points in which there should be full agreement.

1. Though we may differ about this we can still be brethren.

2. No view should lead us to wrong practices.

3. No view should include miracles for us.

4. If a brother differs, we should not attribute to him what he does not believe.

5. We do not learn what to do to be saved and how to live the Christian life from any source but the New Testament.

Of course, we all understand a view is not true just because a respected teacher holds it, but how the Holy Spirit dwells in us is determined only by the Bible (1 Corinthians 4:6). This has been a subject of controversy for centuries, and has been discussed by some deep and scholarly men, so we may not be able to settle it in just a few pages. In fact, what I hope to do in this chapter is to present as clearly as I am able, both views in order to see why faithful brethren have differed on this matter.

PERSONAL INDWELLING

Gift of the Spirit What does it mean "and ye shall receive the gift of the Holy Ghost" (Acts 2:38)? Does it mean you will receive the Holy Spirit as a gift? Or, does it mean you will receive a gift given by the Holy Spirit?

"The expression means the Holy Spirit as a gift; and the reference is to that indwelling of the Holy Spirit by which we bring forth the fruits of the Spirit, and without which we are not of Christ."

---J.W. McGarvey, Commentary on Acts, p 39

"To deny that the Holy Spirit, as a person, dwells in a Christian because he has not been seen of mortal man would be equal to denial of God, whom man has not seen."

- - - V.E. Howard, THE HOLY SPIRIT, p 111

In his lecture on "The Indwelling of the Holy Spirit", John Banister lists seven things the Holy Spirit does for Christians today. (Quotation from THE POWER OF THE HOLY SPIRIT by Batsell Barrett Baxter.)

1. The indwelling of the Holy Spirit is an evidence of our sonship (Galatians 4:6; 1 John 3:24).

2. The indwelling of the Holy Spirit gives strength and help in our Christian living (Ephesians 3:14-16; Romans 8:13).

3. The indwelling of the Holy Spirit means that the Holy Spirit helps us in our prayers (Romans 8:26-27),

4. The indwelling of the Holy Spirit produces good fruit in us (Galatians 5:22—23).

5. The indwelling of the Holy Spirit is an incentive to holiness (1 Corinthians 6:13-20).

6. The indwelling o.f the Holy Spirit inspires hope in us (Romans 15:13).

7. The indwelling of the Holy Spirit is a guarantee or pledge of eternal life (2 Corinthians 5:5).

"The Holy Spirit either (1) really and truly dwells in us——faithful Christians——in a personal manner, or (2) he dwells in us in some other manner, or (3) else he does not dwell in us at all."

---Gus Nichols, LECTURES ON THE HOLY SPIRIT, p 155

Brother Nichols believed number one above, the Holy Spirit dwells in the Christian personally. Pages 155-182 discuss the "Indwelling of the Spirit." I urge you to get a copy of this book if possible.

The following passages are given to show that the Holy Spirit dwells in us (Acts 2:38; 5:32; Romans 8:9—11; 1 Corinthians 3:16; 6:19; 1 Thessalonians 4:8; Jude 19; Ephesians 1:13; 4:30).

Twenty one points are used to build the case for the personal indwelling of the Spirit.

1. Peter used the word "receive" (Acts 2:38). The gift was to be received after repentance and baptism, and after the remission of sins, and was to be received because they obeyed (Acts 5:32).

They received the word before repentance and baptism, and after they had remission of sins. The "gift of the Holy Spirit" followed their receiving the word and is, therefore, something different from receiving the word.

2. Sinners did receive the word before they were saved, but the "gift of the Holy Spirit" is promised after they were saved. Those who were baptized "gladly received the word" (Acts 2:41; 22:16). The gift is promised to those who obey.

3. "The word is received to make one a child of God. The sinner is to be born again 'by the word of God' (1 Peter 1:23; James 1:18; 1 Corinthians 4:15)" (Page 171). After the new birth one is given the spirit (Galatians 4:6). He is given the Spirit, not to make him a child of God, but he is given the Spirit because he is a child of God.

Sinners receive the word before baptism but receive the Spirit after baptism into Christ. In Christ we are "sealed with the Holy Spirit of promise" (Ephesians 1:13).

4. Two questions: a) If God had meant that the Holy Spirit actually dwells in Christians, what other words would He have used to express it? b) Since sinners received the word while they were still sinners, and the gift of the Spirit is promised after baptism, if receiving the Spirit is receiving the word, what is the gift of the Spirit?

5. Brother Nichols does not claim to know the Spirit is in us by feelings or in a miraculous manner. "The only way we can know we have the Spirit is to know we have obeyed the gospel." The only way we can know we have a human spirit in our body is that the Bible reveals it as a fact.

REPRESENTATIVELY THROUGH THE WORD

In a tract "How the Holy Spirit Dwells in the Christian", Guy N. Woods stresses the point that the Holy Spirit teaches and motivates only through the word. He uses the same verses others have used to show the Holy Spirit dwells in us and grants that God, Christ, and the Holy Spirit all dwell in us.

"There is then, a sense in which the Holy Spirit is in us. Such a conclusion, of course, clearly follows. But, do these passages assert the manner or mode of such "indwelling"? No; they assert a fact, but they do not indicate a mode."

---Guy N. Woods, How the Holy Spirit Dwells in Us, p 16

1. If the Holy Spirit dwells personally in a person it is the doctrine of incarnation. The incarnation of Jesus involves His coming in a physical body, so if the Holy Spirit dwells in our bodies now, it is incarnation.

2. When Jesus was on the earth in a body, it was right and proper for people to worship Him. If the Holy Spirit, who is God, dwells in the body of a Christian, then that person would be entitled to worship.

"We believe that the Spirit is in us in precisely the same sense that God, the Father, is in us; we believe the Spirit is in us in precisely the same sense that God, the Son, is in US" (Page 19).

3. God dwells in us through the Spirit (Ephesians 2:22).

4. Christ dwells in us by faith which comes by the word of God (Ephesians 3:17; Romans 10:17). Christ dwells in us through the word.

"It is truly a strange form of exegesis which interprets the scripture which says that the Father and the Son are in us, as indicating a representative indwelling, but which affects to see in a similar passage regarding the Holy Spirit, an actual indwelling. It is a conclusion which results from disregard of the personality of the Holy Spirit" (Page 20).

5. The "gift of the Holy Spirit" in Acts 2:38 and God gives the Spirit to "them that obey" in Acts 5:32, both refer to the miraculous and not to the indwelling of the Spirit.

Acts 2:38 is parallel to Mark 16:16-17 where signs would follow them that believe. These signs came with the laying on of hands of the apostles.

"Because that on the Gentiles also was poured out the gift of the Holy Spirit; for they heard them speak with tongues and magnify God" (Acts 10:45-46). The gift of the Holy Spirit on the Gentiles had the miracle of tongues. The gift of the Holy Spirit in Acts 2:38 is the same kind of gift.

Hardeman-Bogard Debate Brother Hardeman made it clear that the Holy Spirit and the Word work together.

"There is not one thing ever said to be done by God's Spirit but the same thing is said to be done by the word of God. That being true, what is the answer? Just this:

God uses the word as the means by which the Spirit operates. And what one does, the other is said to do--- for they operate together" (Page 43).

"There is no such thing as the Spirit of God operating away or distinct from the written word. Wherever men are converted, the gospel is always there as God's power unto salvation to everyone that believes" (Page 80).

One passage stressed and explained by brother Hardeman in this debate is 2 Corinthians 3:2-3.

"Ye are our epistle written in our hearts, known and read of all men: Forasmuch as ye are manifestly declared to be the epistle of Christ ministered by us, written not with ink, but with the Spirit of the living God; not in tables of stone, but in fleshly tables of the heart."

When truth and error are put side by side, truth will shine and it is easy to see the difference (John 7:17). Notice what both speakers said about this passage in the debate.

Mr. Bogard "In this passage, in conviction and conversion, receiving salvation is compared to writing, only instead of ink the Holy Spirit is the thing that makes the impression. Just as the ink actually touches the paper in order to write, even so the Holy Spirit actually touches the heart, and since the Holy Spirit is as the ink then there must be actual touch by the Holy Spirit on the human heart to produce salvation (page 32)

Brother Hardeman "Ye are our epistle written in our hearts." Now Dr. Bogard, what you really needed is a passage which shows that the writing was done on the

57

sinner's heart. It is in Paul's and Timothy's hearts that this thing was written, "known and read of all men." Now watch: "Ministered by us, written not with ink, but with the Spirit of the living God; not in tables of stone, but in tables that are hearts of flesh." Christ is the writer. The Corinthians themselves are the epistles. The apostle's heart is the paper---not the sinner's heart. The Spirit is the ink, and the apostle represents the pen. Now when Dr. Bogard comes tonight, I want him to bring a fountain pen and show us how the ink writes separate and apart from the pen; whenever he does, I am ready to yield the point. He must find where the ink goes beyond the pen---the preachers of the gospel and their message. Let him show how writing upon the heart out of touch with the pen can be done." (Pages 41-42).

"It should be remembered that the Holy Spirit is never separated from the word of truth in his work of conversion and sanctification."

---H. Leo Boles, THE HOLY SPIRIT, p 206

In his book THE SPIRIT AND THE WORD, Z. T. Sweeney names sixteen things that are claimed for personal indwelling of the Spirit, which are clearly accomplished by the Spirit acting through the word of God.

1. Give us faith (Romans 10:17).
2. Enable us to enjoy a new birth (1 Peter 1:23).
3. Give us light (Psalm 119:130).
4. Give us wisdom (2 Timothy 3:14-15).
5. Convert us (Psalm 19:7).
6. Open our eyes (Psalm 19:8).
7. Give us understanding (Psalm 119:104).
8. Quicken us (Psalm 119:50).

9. Save us (James 1:21).
10. Sanctify us (John 17:17).
11. Purify us (1 Peter 1:22).
12. Cleanse us (John 15:3).
13. Make us free from sin (Romans 6:17-18).
14. Impart a divine nature (2 Peter 1:4).
15. Fit us for glory (Acts 20:32).
16. Strengthen us (Psalm 119:28).

"It is not claimed that direct indwelling of the Spirit makes any new revelations, adds any new reasons or offers any new motives than are found in the word of God. Of what use, then, would a direct indwelling Spirit be?. . .This conclusion is strengthened by the utter absence of any test by which we could know the Spirit dwells in us, if such were the case" (Pages 125- 126).

Then, brother Sweeney names five things the Holy Spirit does for Christians.

1. He is active in our birth (John 3:5; 1 Peter 1:22-23.)
2. He bears witness with our spirit that we are the children of God (Romans 8:16).
3. He makes intercession for us (Romans 8:26).
4. He changes us from glory to glory (2 Corinthians 3:18).
5. He will quicken our mortal bodies (Romans 8:11).

We are told how Christ dwells in us. "That Christ may dwell in your hearts by faith; that ye, being rooted and grounded in love" (Ephesians 3:17). Christ does not dwell in us personally but "by faith". In Romans 10:17 we are told that faith comes by hearing the word of God, which means that as we let the word of God fill our hearts, Christ Is dwelling in our hearts.

In discussing how we grow into a holy temple, Paul says, "In whom ye also are builded together for a habitation of God through the Spirit" (Ephesians 2:22). God dwells in us through the Spirit. Christ dwells in us by faith through the word. Wouldn't it be true that God, Christ, and the Spirit all dwell in us the same way?

QUESTIONS

1. Show from Acts 5:3-4 that the Holy Spirit is God.

2. Study verses that teach the Father, Son, and Holy Spirit dwell in us.

3. What are the two views about how the Holy Spirit dwells in Christians?

4. Discuss five points of agreement before entering a study of how the Holy Spirit dwells in us.

5. Discuss and understand the view of the following in regard to the personal indwelling of the Holy Spirit.

       a. J.W. McGarvey
       b. V.E. Howard
       c. John Banister
       d. Gus Nichols

6. Understand clearly the reasons why Guy N. Woods concludes the Holy Spirit dwells in us representatively through the word.

7. Consider Hardeman-Bogard debate on 2 Corinthians 3:2-3.

8. Study the things listed by Z.T. Sweeney, which the Holy Spirit does, but which the word of God also does.

ALBERT GARDNER

7 THE BOOK WE FOLLOW

The Bible is discredited in the eyes of many today. Bible believers are looked at as being either uneducated or blind. How could anyone in this enlightened age with all of the available knowledge and technology believe the Bible with all its claims and promises?

Most of us have been taught the Bible is from God. My parents instilled this belief in me. Nearly everyone around me in my early life were believers in the Bible, even my public school teachers. But this is not a good enough reason for believing the Bible for we can be taught wrong and led astray. Though we want so much to believe it, are there any good sound reasons for believing the Bible to be the word of God? This is a very serious matter because we have staked our lives, hopes, and dreams on the Bible and what it promises us.

SOME CLAIMS HE BIBLE MAKES ITSELF

We should let the Bible speak on its own behalf. The Bible is accused of many things it does not teach, just as God is blamed for many things He does not do. We need to hear the Bible.

It Claims to be Inspired What Paul received by revelation, he wrote down, and we can read and understand it.

What he wrote was not made known in other ages but is now revealed to the apostles and prophets by the Spirit (Ephesians 3:3-5).

"All Scripture is given by inspiration of God, and is profitable for doctrine, for reproof, for correction, for instruction in righteousness" (2 Timothy 3:16). Concerning the Old Testament, Peter claimed it was inspired. "For the prophecy came not in old time by the will of man: but holy men of God spake as they were moved by the Holy Ghost" (2 Peter 1:21; Acts 1:16; Matthew 22:43; Mark 12:36).

SOME VIEWS OF INSPIRATION

1. It is inspired like Shakespeare, Milton, and others. This would mean it is a purely human book.

2. It is part inspired. That presents a real problem to know which part is inspired, and who is to determine it.

3. It is inspired in thought. God gave the Bible writers a thought and they wrote the book. This would open up the way for many errors.

4. Verbal inspiration. This means the Holy Spirit guarded the Bible writers so they used the right words.

I believe this to be the correct view, for even a letter makes a great difference. 'Now to Abraham and his seed were the promises made. He saIth not, And to seeds, as of many; but as of one, And to thy seed, which is Christ" (Galatians 3:16).

Paul taught verbal inspiration in 1 Corinthians 2:11-13. The reason he received the Spirit was to know the thoughts of God, which he says, he spoke, not in words taught by men but with words taught by the Holy Spirit.

The prophet Jeremiah was told to take a roll and "write therein all the words that I have spoken unto thee" (Jeremiah 36:2). Now, notice what happened to see verbal inspiration at work. "Then Jeremiah called Baruch, the son of Neriah: and Baruch wrote from the mouth of Jeremiah all the words of the Lord, which he had spoken unto him, upon a roll of a book" (verse 4). When asked how he wrote all these things, "Then Baruch answered them, He pronounced all these words unto me with his mouth, and I wrote them with ink in the book" (verse 18). He pronounced the "words" that were given him from God. When God called Jeremiah, He promised him words. "Then the Lord put forth his hand, and touched my mouth. And the Lord said unto me, Behold, I have put my words in thy mouth" (Jeremiah 1:9).

The Bible writers were inspired in the original manuscripts, none of which we have now. We do have copies of the original manuscripts and we have translations from those copies. What about translations? Are they inspired? They are in as much as they are faithful in translation of the Hebrew and Greek words into English.

If you are reading Genesis 1:2 from the New World Translation by the Jehovah Witnesses, it is not inspired when it calls the Holy Spirit "an active force." The Spirit is a person who can speak (1 Timothy 4:1), can be grieved (Ephesians 4:30), and is God (Acts 5:3-4). If you are reading Acts 12:4 from the King James Version where it uses the word Easter, it is not inspired for the context shows it should read passover. If you are reading Acts 8:38 from Goodspeed's translation, it is not inspired when it says that Philip and the eunuch stopped the car. That is just too modern since the automobile began in the twentieth century.

When the translators give us an English word that is equivalent to the Hebrew or Greek word, it is a faithful translation and is, therefore, inspired.

It Claims to be the Truth Since only the truth makes men free, we should be deeply interested in knowing only truth (Proverbs 23:23; John 8:32). Pilate asked, "What is truth?" (John 18:38). Jesus included the answer to that question in His prayer. "Sanctify them through thy truth: thy word is truth" (John 17:17).

It Claims We Are To Live By It When Satan asked Jesus to command the stone to be made bread, He replied: "Man shall not live by bread alone, but by every word that proceedeth out of the mouth of God" (Matthew 4:4). Our Lord said we are to "live" by the word of God.

It Claims To Be the Standard of Judgment "He that rejecteth me, and receiveth not my words, hath one that judgeth him: the word that I have spoken, the same shall judge him in the last day" (john 12:48). "And I saw the dead, small and great stand before God; and the books were opened: and another book was opened, which is the book of life: and the dead were judged out of those things which were written in the books, according to their works" (Revelation 20:12). "The books were opened" I believe to be the sixty six books of our Bible. Those who lived under the Old Testament will be judged by it and those who lived under the New Testament will be judged by it.

WHY WE BELIEVE THE BIBLE

The claims are valid only if the Bible is true. We now look at some powerful evidence for the Bible. (I urge you to read WHY WE BELIEVE THE BIBLE, by George W. DeHoff, DeHoff Publications, Murfreesboro, TN. It is an outstanding defense of the Bible.)

We Believe the Bible Because of the Unity Between Bible and Science

The Bible is not a science book but when it makes a scientific statement, it is always up to date. It is not a geography book but it is always geographically correct. When it makes a historical statement it is always true.

1. **Blood** In telling, about the greatness and power of God when Paul preached the Unknown God sermon, he

said He "hath made of one blood all nations of men for to dwell on all the face of the earth, and hath determined the times before appointed, and the bounds of their habitation (Acts 17:26).

In 1960 I wrote the following letter to J. Edgar Hoover.

May 30, 1960

Mr. J. Edgar Hoover
Federal Bureau of Investigation
Washington, D.C.

Dear Sir:

Since your Laboratory is so complete and reliable may I have the answers to the following questions?

1. Is there a difference in the blood of animals and man?

2. Is there a difference in the blood of a monkey and man?

3. Is there a difference in the blood of the different nations of people? For instance, is the blood of the Negro and the blood of the white man the same?

Thank you for your kindness.

Sincerely,

Albert Gardner

In a very short time I received the following reply.

June 8, 1960

Mr. Albert Gardner
116 Hawkins Street
Vicksburg, Mississippi

Dear Mr. Gardner:

Your letter dated May 30, 1960, has been received, and your kind remarks concerning our FBI Laboratory are appreciated.

In response to your questions, I would like to advise that there is a difference between the blood of human beings and that of animals, including monkeys, and the difference can be detected through laboratory analysis if the conditions are suitable. The tests employed in the FBI Laboratory are primarily for the determination of whether a bloodstain is of human or animal origin. We are unable to furnish any information relating to similarities or differences of racial origin.

Sincerely yours,

S/ John Edgar Hoover
    Director

This is in complete agreement with the statement Paul made in Acts 17:26, that God has made of one blood all nations of men. We have a different blood than the animals, including monkeys. That means we did not come from them for our blood is different. What evolutionists believe about it is wrong.

Not only do we have different blood, we have different flesh. "All flesh is not the same flesh: but there is one kind of flesh of men, another flesh of beasts, another of fishes, and another of birds" (1 Corinthians 15:39). We did not evolve from the animals for we do not have the same blood or the same flesh, but we were both created by the living God (Genesis 1:24-27).

With modern technology they are learning more and more about the blood but they will continue to confirm what the Bible has said all along, that we are of one blood. The Bible is not a science book but whenever it makes a scientific statement, it is always up to date and true.

This causes us to have confidence in the Bible, for it reveals a scientific truth that has taken us centuries to learn. How did Paul know we are of one blood? He was not a doctor or a scientist, but was a tentmaker. He had to have more than human wisdom to state this fact. This adds credibility to his claim in 1 Corinthians 2:13, that he spoke not with words of men but by words taught to him by the Holy Spirit. The Bible is right.

2. **Germs** In Leviticus 13 and 14, Moses gives details about how leprosy was detected by the priest and what was to be done. If it looked a certain way, the person would be shut up for a week and re-examined. If he were not improved he would be shut up for another week.

Some years ago people were "quarantined when they had diseases that could spread with contact. Now we call it "isolation" when they are in the hospital. We have learned that some diseases can be "caught" or transmitted by contact, so people are separated from other people in order to prevent an epidemic. With our modern technology we have learned about germs and viruses, but how did Moses know anything about them? He took care of sheep for forty years and was certainly not a scientist. His writing about disease is in complete agreement with modern science.

3. **Shape of the earth** "It is he that sitteth upon the circle of the earth, and the inhabitants thereof are as grasshoppers; that stretcheth out the heavens as a curtain, and spreadeth them out as a tent to dwell in" (Isaiah 40:22).

Almost eight hundred years before Christ, Isaiah wrote about the circle of the earth. Only in recent times have people concluded that the earth is round. In the time of Columbus, many thought the earth was flat and that if you went so far you would just fall off and never be heard of again. The Bible does refer to the "four corners" of the earth (Revelation 7:1), but this refers to the different directions and not to the shape of it. It strengthens our faith in Isaiah, that by revelation he could write this in his time.

4. **Suspension of the earth** "He stretcheth out the north over the empty place, and hangeth the earth upon nothing" (Job 26:7). Only in recent times have we learned about gravity. Those who go into space know that they have to get away from the pull of gravity and come into it when they return to earth.

In some places there is the belief that the earth is on the back of a giant turtle, while some have believed it was on the shoulders of Atlas. Now we know that the law of gravity is involved and that the earth is suspended and hangs on nothing.

We know that, but how did Job know it? Job may be the oldest Bible book, so where did he learn something so long ago that has only been recently discovered?

5. **Empty place in the north** (Job 26:7) Job tells us there is an empty place in the north. In recent years, astronomers have turned their powerful telescopes to the north and found an empty place. There are no stars.

Job does not give a reason for this empty place but informs us that it is there. How did he know more than our modern astronomers with advanced telescopes? Revelation is the only adequate answer.

6. **Paths in the Seas** Matthew Fontaine Murray had his son read to him from Psalm 8. He observed especially, verse 8, which says God has given man dominion over "the fowl of the air, and the fish of the sea, and whatsoever passeth through the paths of the seas." Murray said if God says there are paths in the seas that he would find them. He did find them and charted them and they are used by the ocean going vessels today.

Hos did David know there are paths in the seas? He was not a sailor. He was a shepherd, yet he gave a scientific truth that took centuries for men to find, though the Bible had said it all the time. David wrote by the Holy Spirit (Acts 1:16).

7. **The Ark and Ships** In 1919 the U.S. launched its first concrete ship. It was not the same size as the ark but the proportions were the same. It was 300 by 50 by 30. Of course, Noah was told how to make the ark and the size of it.

When the Bible makes a historical, geographical, or scientific statement, it will always be in keeping with the true findings of modern science and technology.

We Believe the Bible Because of the Internal Evidence

The Bible is one of the best arguments for the inspiration and credibility of the Bible. It was written over a period of 1600 years and there is not a contradiction in it, yet there is a unity that cannot be explained naturally. When books are written today, even the same author may not agree with what he wrote ten years ago because of later information which was not available when the first book was written. Bible writers never find themselves in this dilemma. Since the writers were separated by many years this prevented a conspiracy on what to write.

"And the Scripture, foreseeing that God would justify the heathen through faith, preached before the gospel unto Abraham, saying, In thee shall all nations be blessed" (Galatians 3:8). Paul says the Scripture was "foreseeing" this. Only God could foresee because we don't even know what a day will bring forth. Every error that has ever been taught or ever will be taught, inside or outside the church, has already been condemned in the Bible.

It is not by chance that so much is stated in the Bible about baptism being a burial (Romans 6:3-5; Matthew 3:16; John 3:23). The Holy Spirit knew that people would teach the error that baptism can be done by sprinkling.

It is not an accident that Matthew 8:14 mentions Peter's wife's mother and that Peter said he was an elder (1

Peter 5:1), which means he was married and had children. God knew that down the way somebody would teach that Peter was a Pope.

There is purpose behind the Bible. There are no fillers or unnecessary verses.

We Believe the Bible Because Archaeology Confirms it

Archaeology does not prove the Bible but confirms it. When a city mentioned in the Bible is uncovered, they will learn how things were. What they find will be in agreement with the Bible account.

When the children of Israel were in Egypt as slaves, they were required to make a certain number of bricks each day to build Pithom and Raamses, treasure cities for Pharaoh. When Moses asked Pharaoh to let the people go, Pharaoh asked the taskmasters to increase the work on the people because he said they were idle and that was the reason they wanted to go worship God. The way they did that is stated in Exodus 5:7. "Ye shall no more give the people straw to make brick, as heretofore: let them go and gather straw for themselves." They were required to make the same number of bricks and gather straw too.

The result could almost be predicted. "So the people were scattered abroad throughout all the land of Egypt to gather stubble instead of straw" (Exodus 5:12).

The walls of the city of Pithom have been found and they tell the story. If the Bible account is true, we would expect them to find exactly what they did.

"Naville, 1883, and Kyle, 1908, found at Pithom, the lower courses of brick filled with good chopped straw; the middle course, with less straw, and that was stubble plucked up by the root; and the upper courses of brick were of pure clay, having no straw whatever. What an amazing confirmation of the Exodus account!"
---Henry H. Halley, BIBLE HANDBOOK, P. 117

Since what they found confirms the Bible account, we accept the Bible as being truthful and is authoritative.

We Believe the Bible Because of Fulfilled Prophecy

We do not mean by prophecy some simple prediction based on current evidence. If one looks at the clouds and sees the lightning and hears the thunder, he may say, "1 think it is going to rain." One would be rather dense not to think that under those conditions. But the Bible prophets had no such evidence.

How could Isaiah, some eight hundred years before the event, know that Jesus would be speechless to Pilate (John 19:9), and that He would die with the wicked and be buried with the rich (Isaiah 53:7,9)? There was nothing around the prophet that would lead him to think that. He could not have given this prophecy by human wisdom.

How could Micah, some seven centuries before Christ, know that Jesus would be born in Bethlehem? He stated this in Micah 5:2, and it happened in Luke 2:4-7.

<u>QUESTIONS</u>

1. Discuss some different views of inspiration, especially studying 1 Corinthians 2:11-13.

2. See how Jeremiah 36 is an example of verbal inspiration.

3. Name and discuss some claims the Bible makes for itself.

4. Discuss the unity of true science and the Bible.

5. Give some internal evidence for belief in the Bible.

6. How does archaeology confirm the Bible?

7. Consider the nature of prophecy and why we can believe the Bible because of fulfilled prophecy.

8 WHAT ABOUT THE APOCRYPHA?

Because there were many uninspired accounts of the life of Christ, Luke saw the need of writing an authentic account free from error which would be authoritative.

"It seemed good to me also, having had perfect understanding of all things from the very first, to write unto thee in order most excellent Theophilus, that thou mightest know the certainty of those things, wherein thou hast been instructed" (Luke 1:3-4).

Though he was not an apostle, he was an inspired prophet in which we can have complete confidence (Ephesians 3:5).

WHAT IS THE CANON?

The canon is the authoritative list of books accepted as Holy Scripture. The word canon came from words that mean rule, model, or standard. The canon is made up of books which serve as a standard of judgment and manner of life.

The books which are not included in the Bible are said to be apocryphal. They are books of doubtful authenticity; spurious.

The Roman Catholic Bible contains nine apocryphal books which are not in the King James and later translations. In the Council of Laodicea A.D. 363, the Greek branch denied that the apocryphal books were inspired, and prohibited their use in churches. The Council of Trent, on April 8, 1546, under the direction of the pope, declared tradition and the apocrypha to be canonical and authoritative; and hence these apocryphal books are always found in Roman Catholic Bibles.

One council said they should be a part of the Bible and another council says they are not a part of the Bible. A book is not inspired because a council voted it that way, for this in no way changes the character of the book. It is either inspired or it isn't. Taking lead and stamping it 14K gold does not change its nature for it is still lead. Luther said, "The church cannot give more force or authority to a book than it has in itself. A council cannot make that to be Scripture which in its own nature is not Scripture."
        ---Sidney Collett, ALL ABOUT THE BIBLE, p. 58

HOW WAS THE CANON SET?

Who determined what books should be in the Bible? On what basis were they accepted or rejected? Are there lost books? Can we be sure we have all the Scriptures? These are important questions, which need to be answered if our faith in the Bible is to continue to grow.

All twenty-seven books we have in our New Testament, were listed and acknowledged as genuine, in the Council of Carthage in A. D. 397. Ezra is believed to have arranged all the books of the Old Testament in order about 457 B. C. (except Nehemiah and Malachi, which were written later).

Collett's Answer "How, then, was this all-important matter settled? It was decided by the internal testimony and intrinsic value of the writings themselves--- just as the true character of a tree, though questioned, and even vehemently denied, for a time in the dead months of winter, will, nevertheless, soon be established beyond all doubt---not on the authority of some expert gardener or association of gardeners, but by its own unanswerable evidence in the flower and fruit it bears." pp.58-59

The book itself determines whether it should be in the Bible. By just reading the book of John and a novel, one can tell the difference. The Bible is different, and that difference is obvious. Regardless who collected the books the first time, it must be on the basis of the content, claims, and nature of the book itself.

Lost Books "And when this epistle is read among you, cause that it be read also in the church of the

Laodiceans; and that ye likewise read the epistle from Laodicea" (Colossians 4:16).

We do not have a letter to the church of the Laodiceans, though some believe the book of Ephesians is that letter, and that Ephesians should be named Laodicean. If that is not true, then, we can be sure we do not need it because it would have contained the same material included in the books of Colossians and Ephesians.

"I wrote unto you in an epistle not to company with fornicators" (1 Corinthians 5:9). This would mean Paul wrote them a letter before he wrote the one we call First Corinthians. We do not have three books to them. It has not been preserved because the needed information is included in what we call First Corinthians.

God's Part in the Canon The promise that His word would not pass away but would abide for ever (1 Peter 1:25), and that He has "given unto us all things that pertain unto life and godliness" (2 Peter 1:3), is proof that no part of the Scripture is lost or has been left out.

Concerning the works of Christ, we are told that we do not have all of them written down.

"And many other signs truly did Jesus in the presence of his disciples, which are not written in this book: but these are written, that ye might believe that Jesus is the Christ, the Son of God; and that believing ye might have life through his name" (John 20:30-31).

We have enough of His signs recorded to produce faith that will save us. But there is a practical reason why everything has not been included in the Bible.

"And there are also many other things which Jesus did, the which, if they should be written every one, I suppose that even the world itself could not contain the books that should be written" (John 21:25).

If every detail in the life of Jesus, and all of the letters written by Paul and others (which were repetitious), were recorded, we would need a truck to carry the New Testament. We could not have a copy of the entire New Testament to put in pocket or purse. It would be so big and bundlesome that it would be unusable, for we could never find the verse we needed.

REASONS THE APOCRYPHA IS REJECTED

Neil Lightfoot, in HOW WE GOT THE BIBLE, pp. 71-73, gives the following as reasons for not accepting the apocrypha.

1. These books were never included in the Hebrew canon of the Old Testament.

2. These books, as far as the evidence goes, were never accepted as canonical by Jesus and His apostles.

3. These books were not accepted as Scripture by such Jewish writers of the first century as Philo and Josephus, Origin, and Jerome (A. D. 400 Jerome translated Latin Vulgate).

4. These books do not evidence intrinsic qualities of inspiration.

5. These books have been shrouded with continual uncertainty.

6. These books cannot be maintained on a compromise basis. Church of England gives to the apocrypha a semi-canonical status. They may be read in public worship "for example of life and instruction of manners" but not in order "to establish any doctrine."

7. Objections to these books cannot be overruled by dictatorial authority. On April 8, 1546, in the Fourth Session of the Council of Trent, the Roman Catholic Church pronounced the Old Testament Apocrypha as authoritative and canonical Scripture.

Henry C. Thiessen, in INTRODUCTION TO THE NEW TESTAMENT, p.10, gives four things which aided in the determination of which books should be accepted as canonical. They are: apostolicity, contents, universality, and inspiration.

Another list of reasons which the author has collected from unknown sources may include some of the above reasons.

1. Jesus never accepted them.
2. Jesus never referred to them.
3. New Testament writers never quote from them.
4. Some stories in them are too ludicrous to be taken seriously.
5. It contains error. 2 Maccabees 12:42 teaches prayer for the dead; purgatory.

6. No essential doctrine is contributed by them.

7. Vulgate and Jerome excluded them.

QUESTIONS

1. Why did Luke say he wanted to write the book of Luke?

4. Can a council make a book Holy Scripture?

5. How was the canon set? Notice Collett's answer.

6. Are there "lost" books? Consider Colossians 4:16 and 1 Corinthians 5:9.

7. Consider a practical reason why every detail of the life of Christ is not recorded.

8. Study one by one, the lists of reasons we do not accept the apocrypha.

ALBERT GARDNER

9 THE CHURCH HE BOUGHT

The church is very important when one sees it the way God sees it. In Matthew 16:18 is the first time the word church is used in the New Testament. "And I say also unto thee, That thou art Peter, and upon this rock I will build my church; and the gates of hell shall not prevail against it."

In the beginning of this study, we must identify just which church it is that we are discussing. There are hundreds of churches in existence, which wear different names, teach different doctrines, and have different practices. We do not use the word church to mean all of them combined. We do not use the word church to refer to any particular denomination, but to the church mentioned in the Bible.

When Jesus promised to build His church, He said the gates of hell would not prevail against it. Notice two words in this verse. "Church" is singular and "it" means one. Our Lord promised and did build only one church. All other churches developed later. "And gave him to be the head over all things to the church, which is his body" (Ephesians 1:22- 23). Since the church is the body, if we can find out how many bodies, we will know how many churches. In Ephesians 4:4-6, there are seven things listed of which there is only one. "There is one body, and one Spirit, even as ye are called in one hope of your calling; one Lord, one faith, one baptism, one God and Father of all, who is above all, and through all, and in you all." Notice, there is one body. What is the body? It is the church. So, how many churches are there revealed in the Bible? There are as many bodies or churches as there are Gods, or Holy Spirits, or Lord Jesus Christs. Of course, there are many gods now. But the apostle Paul means there is only one loving, holy, all-wise, all-powerful God. In the same way, he means there is only one body that wears the right name, worships the right way, and teaches the right thing. It is this church we are discussing now.

THINGS WHICH SHOW THE IMPORTANCE THE CHURCH

1. **The church was in the mind of God before the world was** "To the intent that now unto the principalities and powers in heavenly places might be known by the church the manifold wisdom of God, according to the eternal purpose which he purposed in Christ Jesus our Lord." Before the foundation of the world the church was in the mind of God, and it was planned that Jesus would die

for it. "Who verily was foreordained before the foundation of the world, but was manifest in these last times for you" (1 Peter 1:20).

2. **The church is included in the promise of God** Abraham was told that through his seed the whole world would be blessed. "Now to Abraham and his seed were the promises made. He saith not, And to seeds, as of many; but as of one, And to thy seed, which is Christ" (Galatians 3:16).

3. **The church was a subject of prophecy** Nearly 800 years before Christ, Isaiah foretold the church. "And it shall come to pass in the last days, that the mountain of the Lord's house shall be established in the top of the mountains, and shall be exalted above the hills; and all nations shall flow unto it" (Isaiah 2:2). He said the "Lord's house" would be built. The New Testament reveals what the Lord's house means. "But if I tarry long, that thou mayest know how thou oughtest to behave thyself in the house of God, which is the church of the living God, the pillar and ground of the truth" (1 Timothy 3:15). The house of God is the church of the living God. The prophet was talking about the church being established hundreds of years before it actually came to pass.

4. **John the baptist prepared the way for the church** He was preaching "repent for the kingdom is at hand." John fulfilled prophecy in doing this. "For this is he that was spoken of by the prophet Isaiah, saying, The voice of one crying in the wilderness. Prepare ye the way of the Lord, make his paths straight" (Matthew 3:3).

5. **The church began on Pentacost** From Matthew 16:18 onward, the church is spoken of as being in

the future, until we come to Acts 2:47. "And the Lord added to the church daily such as should be saved." From this time forward the church is in existence.

DEPARTURES

Though Satan could not prevail against the building of the church, he set out to destroy it in every possible way. One way he tried this was to multiply churches. He has made so many churches that people are confused and wonder which one is right. It is like a counterfeiter of money or of a great painting. The nearer he comes to the original, the more dangerous and deceptive his work becomes. It is like that in religion. The more like the true church it is, yet lacking some essential qualities, the more deceptive it is.

Departures were foretold in Scripture. "Now the Spirit speaketh expressly, that in the latter times some shall depart from the faith, giving heed to seducing spirits, and doctrines of devils; speaking lies in hypocrisy; having their conscience seared with a hot iron; forbidding to marry, and commanding to abstain from meats, which God hath created to be received with thanksgiving of them which believe and know the truth (1 Timothy 4:1-3).

"Let no man deceive you by any means: for that day shall not come, except there come a falling away first, and that man of sin be revealed, the son of perdition; who opposeth and exalteth himself above all that is called God, or that is worshiped; so that he as God sitteth in the temple of God, showing himself that he is God" (2 Thessalonians 2:3-4).

In talking with the elders from Ephesus, the apostle said, "For I know this, that after my departing shall grievous wolves enter in among you, not sparing the flock. Also of your own selves shall men arise, speaking perverse things, to draw away disciples after them" (Acts 20:28).

There would be so many departures in names they wore, the worship they offered, the teaching they gave, and in the government or organization of the church---that it actually became another church. This is how the Roman Catholic Church developed, and all Protestant denominations developed later.

HOW CAN WE FIND THE RIGHT ONE?

How would you find an animal that was lost? You would get a description of it, such as kind, size and color. If a cow is lost, one would not go in search of a horse. If a black horse is lost, one need not consider a white one.

When there are so many churches, one would need a description of the right one from the Bible. Just because one is religious, or even sincere, does not make one right. Jesus said, "Not every one that saith unto me, Lord, Lord, shall enter into the kingdom of heaven; but he that doeth the will of my Father which is in heaven" (Matthew 7:21). What can we learn from the Bible which will enable us to identity the church of Christ?

1. **Names** It is called the "church of God" (1 Corinthians 1:2). Actually, that is not the name of it but a term which shows ownership. It is the church "of" God because He planned it. It is the "church of Christ" (Romans 16:16). It is the church "of" Christ because He purchased it

with His own blood (Acts 20:28). It is the body of Christ (Ephesians 1:22-23). It is the household or family of God (Galatians 6:10). It is the kingdom of God (John 3:3).

These are terms that tell more what the church is and who it belongs to rather than a name for it, but one would know immediately that a church named after a man such as Luther, or one named after a doctrine like baptism, is not the one revealed in the Bible, for it has the wrong name.

2. **Date** When was it started? The one Jesus said He would build, began on the first Pentecost following the resurrection of Christ, in A.D.33, and is recorded in Acts 2.

A church that developed through departures from the original one and became full grown by A.D. 606 could not be considered. One that did not start until 1500 and after is not the one we are searching for.

3. **Place** Where did it start? Prophecy stated it would begin in Jerusalem (Isaiah 2:3), and that is the exact place it did begin.

What about churches that began in Rome, Germany, England or some other place? It is clear that the church of Christ began in Jerusalem.

4. **Founder and Head** Jesus said, "I will build my church" (Matthew 16:18). He did build it and is the head of it. "And he is the head of the body, the church" (Colossians 1:18).

Churches have been started by Luther, Calvin, Wesley, and King Henry the eighth. All of them have some person as the head of them now. There are not two heads;

one in heaven and one on earth. That would make the one body having two heads! Jesus is the true head of the true church.

5. **<u>Organization or government</u>** The church has Jesus as its head and has elders and deacons in every church (Philippians 1:1; Acts 14:23). Each congregation has elders to oversee the work and worship of one church, and has no authority over another. The words "elder" and "bishop" refer to the same person or office (Titus 1:5 elder; verse 7 bishop).

Councils, conventions, and synods are without Bible authority. One person over several churches is contrary to Scripture. To be the church of Christ, it must have the right organization.

6. **<u>Worship</u>** The New Testament church met on the first day of the week to eat the Lord's Supper (Acts 20:7); to give of their income to do the work of the church (1 Corinthians 16:2); pray (Acts 2:42); sing (Ephesians 5:19); and hear the gospel preached (Acts 20:7).

Often people say they eat the Lord's Supper once in a month, or once every three months, or once in a year. The pattern for the church calls for eating the Lord's Supper each first day of the week.

7. **<u>What must I do to be saved?</u>** What are sinners to do to be saved? What must one do to become a member of the church? The answers to these questions will not be found in the practices or doctrines of men but only in the New Testament. The first day the church existed is recorded

in Acts 2. We should find the answer to these questions by seeing what they did then.

Peter taught about the death, burial, and resurrection of our Lord, and told them that He had ascended back to His Father and was seated at His right hand. His sermons brought them to the main point in Acts 2:36. "Therefore let all the house of Israel know assuredly, that God hath made that same Jesus, whom ye crucified, both Lord and Christ."

They now believe that Jesus Christ is the Son of God, for when they heard Peter's sermon "they are pricked in their heart, and said unto Peter and to the rest of the apostles, Men and brethren, what shall we do?" We must notice carefully what they were told to do.

"Then Peter said unto them, Repent, and be baptized every one of you in the name of Jesus Christ for the remission of sins, and ye shall receive the gift of the Holy Ghost" (Acts 2:38). Believers in Christ as the Son of God are told to repent and be baptized for the remission or forgiveness of their sins.

What did they do to become members of the church? Verse 41 says about 3,000 gladly received the word and were baptized. Verse 47 says "And the Lord added to the church daily such as should be saved." The Lord adds the saved to the church. One does not do one thing to be saved and something else to get into the church. When a believer repents and is baptized, he is saved and the Lord adds him to the church.

A church that will not teach the truth about what to do to be saved and how to get into the church is not the one we are searching for, since this is one way we can identify it.

How can we locate the church of Christ among the hundreds of churches today? There are three ways.

1. **Get a Bible description of it** Find out what names it wore, the date it started, the place it began, who started it and who is its head, know the organization it had, see what they did in worship, and find out what they were told to do to be saved and how they became members of the church. Then, make proper application for today.

2. **Follow the pattern** When Moses was about to make the tabernacle he was told to build according to the pattern (Hebrews 8:5). This is true with the church. We find out how they worshipped and worship that way. We see what they taught and practiced and we do the same. We learn what they taught about salvation and that is what we teach.

3. **Sow the same seed** In the beginning of the world a principle was established that "everything will bring forth after its kind." This is not only true in nature but is also true in spiritual matters. "Be not deceived; God Is not mocked: for whatsoever a man soweth, that shall he also reap" (Galatians 6:7). Let us see how this works.

Suppose there is no church of Christ in this city but we want to start one. How would we go about it? We would sow the same seed that was used to bring the church into existence the first time. We do not need a succession of churches to have it. If there is no wheat in your country, and you wanted a wheat harvest, how would you have one? You would get the seed and plant it and it would produce wheat. It will never produce something else.

If we follow the events of the Day of Pentecost in Acts 2, we will 1) see that people were convinced they were sinners 2) they were told of a crucified and resurrected Saviour, which proved Jesus to be the Son of God, 3) they believed and asked what to do to be saved, 4) they are told to repent and be baptized for the remission of their sins, and 5) upon doing this they are added to the church.

If we teach the same thing today, people believe it and obey it, and the Lord adds them to the church, to which church will they be added? If you do the same things the people on Pentecost did, why won't you be a member of the same church they were members of? If you become a member of a different church, a different seed was sown and accepted.

THE DESTINY OF THE CHURCH

It is important that you are a member of the church of Christ because of its destiny. Jesus is the "savior of the body" (Ephesians 5:23). "Then cometh the end, when he shall have delivered up the kingdom to God, even the Father; when he shall have put down all rule and all authority and power" (1 Corinthians 15:24).

After we become Christians, we are to be faithful unto death (Revelation 2:10).

QUESTIONS

1. Discuss the origin, nature, and beginning of the church.

2. Discuss five things which show the importance God places on the church.

3. Study 1 Timothy 4:1-3; 2 Thessalonians 2:3-4 and Acts 20:28-30.

4. Name and discuss seven identifying marks of the church.

5. Give the principle of following a pattern and sowing the seed.

6. What is the destiny of the church?

ALBERT GARDNER

10 THE SALVATION HE GIVES

Instead of the popular expression "we need a personal relationship with Jesus", the Bible uses such words as "saved", "justified' and "redeemed."

Nothing is more important than our salvation, for the very reason we exist is to find and serve God (Acts 17:27). "For God hath not appointed us to wrath, but to obtain salvation by our Lord Jesus Christ" (1 Thessalonians 5:9). We were appointed to be saved, so if we are unsaved and die lost, we will have failed in our purpose for being here.

ORIGINAL SIN

The doctrine of "original sin" is the teaching that we are born guilty of Adam's sin; that biologically the guilt of Adam's sin is transmitted to our children. There are some compelling reasons why this doctrine is untrue.

1. Passages used to teach it, say what the condition is, not how they were born (Romans 3:12).

2. Sin cannot be inherited because of what sin is (1 John 3:4; James 4:17).

3. Sin cannot be inherited because we do not get our spirit from our parents (Acts 17:28; Ecclesiastes 12:7; Zechariah 12:1; Hebrews 12:9).

4. The Bible holds each person responsible for his actions (Acts 2:38; 2 Corinthians 5:10).

That we are guilty of sin none can deny, but it is our own sin and not the sin of others that separate us from God (Isaiah 59:2; Romans 3:23; 1 John 1:8—10).

CONSEQUENCES vs GUILT

We do suffer some consequences of Adam's sin but not the guilt of it. Often people suffer for the sins of another. Drinking alcohol by the mother can cause defects in her unborn baby. Who would say the baby is guilty? A drunken driver can kill or cripple innocent people. They are not guilty but suffer the consequences of the sin of another. Someone may kill a Head of State and the whole nation will suffer, but the people do not bear guilt in the crime but they suffer the consequences of it.

So it is with Adam' sin. We will die a physical death as one of the consequences of his sin. "For as in Adam all die, even so in Christ shall all be made alive" (1 Corinth ians 15:22). Death is an appointment all will keep (Hebrews 9:27). We have had the misfortune of being born outside the Garden of Eden and away from the tree of life, which means physical death is passed on us as a consequences of Adam's sin.

The doctrine of original sin requires that we inherit the guilt of Adam's sin. A clear distinction must be made between the guilt and consequences of sin if we are to arrive at truth on this subject. One consequence of our sins is spiritual death (Romans 6:23), but the guilt is not that of another but our own guilt.

HOPE OF ETERNAL LIFE

The claim is often made for the present possession of eternal life. If this is true, it would follow that one could not be lost after having been saved, for if one could lose it, it would not be "eternal" life he had. This is the source of the doctrine "once-in-grace-always-in-grace." What is it we have? Do we have eternal life now?

Present and Future There is a present salvation and a future salvation. After the rich young ruler went away unsaved, the apostles "were astonished out of measure, saying among themselves, Who then can be saved?" Peter made a personal application of what Jesus said, and claimed they had left all in order to follow Jesus. In other words, "we have left all, now what is there in it for us?"

Jesus replied, "But he shall receive a hundredfold now in this time, houses, and brethren, and sisters, and mothers, and children, and lands, with persecutions; and in the world to come eternal life" (Mark 10:30).

Please notice "ye shall receive a hundredfold now in this time." This is present salvation. "And in the world to come eternal life." That is future salvation. When one is baptized according to Mark 16:16, he is saved. He has present salvation, and after a faithful life he will have eternal life which is future salvation.

Paul also recognizes this difference. "For bodily exercise profiteth little: but godliness is profitable unto all things, having promise of the life that now is, and of that which is to come" (1 Timothy 4:8). Promise of "the life that now is", obviously is present salvation. The life which is to come is future salvation.

Hope of Eternal Life "For we are saved by hope: but hope that is seen is not hope: for what a man seeth, why doth he yet hope for?" (Romans 8:24). Paul makes it clear that if we already have it, then we don't hope for it but it is seen as a reality. We are saved by hope, so in some sense we do not possess salvation now.

The sense in which we have eternal life is the promise of it or the hope of it. "And for this cause he is the mediator of the new testament, that by means of death, for the redemption of the transgressions that were under the first testament, they which are called might receive the promise of eternal inheritance" (Hebrews 9:15). We have the promise of eternal life on conditions which all must meet.

"In hope of eternal life, which God, that cannot lie, promised before the world began" (Titus 1:2). Since we do not possess eternal life but have the promise or hope of it, the "once-in-grace-always-in-grace" doctrine can find no comfort in these verses. It means we can live in such a way as to lose our present salvation and forfeit the hope of future salvation.

Hebrews 3:12 is written to "brethren." These are people who have been saved. "Take heed, brethren, lest there be in any of you an evil heart of unbelief, in departing from the living God." Is it possible for a brother to be saved with an "evil heart of unbelief"? Can one be saved who has departed from the living God? They have lost present salvation and they no longer have the hope of eternal life. Of course, they can regain it by repentance, confession, and prayer (Acts 8:22; 1 John 1:9).

Peter refers to eternal life as an inheritance. "To an inheritance incorruptible, and undefiled, and that fadeth not away, reserved in heaven for you" (1 Peter 1:4). One does not have eternal life now for it is reserved in heaven for us. We do hope for it.

SALVATION BOTH HUMAN DIVINE

The question "What must I do to be saved?", is both active and passive. "What must I do?" is active. There are some things I must do, and no one can do them for me. If we don't have to do anything, then, everyone would be saved. Since God is no respecter of persons, if there are no conditions of salvation, God would save everyone, something He says He will not do (John 5:28-29).

The question is also passive. "What must I do to be saved?" There are some things I cannot do for myself, which God will do for me. This means salvation is both human and divine.

DIVINE PART
1. We are saved by grace (Ephesians 2:8-9).
2. We are saved by mercy (Titus 3:5).
3. We are saved by love (John 3:16).
4. We are saved by hope (Romans 8:24).
5. We are saved by the gospel (Romans 1:16).
6. We are saved by blood (Revelation 1:5).
7. We are saved by the resurrection (1 Corinthians 15:1-4).

HUMAN PART
1. We are saved by faith (Hebrews 11:6).
2. We are saved by repentance (Acts 17:30).
3. We are saved by confession (Romans 10:10; Matthew 10:32).
4. We are saved by baptism (Mark 16:16; 1 Peter 3:21).
5. We are saved by obedience (Matthew 7:21; Hebrews 5:8-9).
6. We are saved by works (James 2:24).
7. We save ourselves (Acts 2:40).

"Wherefore that we are justified by faith only is a most wholesome doctrine, and very full of comfort.
---Methodist Discipline, 1960, p. 32

This doctrine is more widely accepted and vigorously taught over the entire world than any other false doctrine. The New Testament uses the words "faith" and "only" one time together. "Ye see then how that by works a man is justified, and not by faith only" (James 2:24).

Others teach we are saved "wholly" by grace. We are saved by grace but not grace only. We are saved by faith but not faith only. In fact, we are not saved by anything "only". Salvation is attributed to many things both human and divine.

SALVATION BEFORE AND AFTER THE CROSS

The cross is the dividing line of history. The law was nailed to the cross (Colossians 2:14). If we go back to the law to bind it upon people now, we are obligated to take the whole law (Galatians 5:3-4). This would include the penalties for breaking the law, animal sacrifices, and going to Jerusalem for three annual feasts. God took away the first that He might establish the second, and by it we are saved (Hebrews 10:9-10).

While Jesus lived on the earth He saved people on terms stated by Him at the time, but when He died His last will and testament went into force (Hebrews 9:16-17). Conditions of salvation were not the same in each case, but He had the right and power to do that during His life time. After His death, and from Pentecost in Acts 2, the requirements have been the same for everyone.

Before the Cross Zaccheus was told, "This day is salvation come to this house, forasmuch as he also is a son of Abraham (Luke 19:9).

The palsied man was brought to Jesus by four, and "when Jesus saw their faith, he said unto the sick of the palsy, Son, thy sins be forgiven thee" (Mark 2:5).

The thief on the cross was told "Today shalt thou be with me in paradise (Luke 23:43).

The rich young ruler was told to sell what he had, give it to the poor, and take up the cross and follow Jesus (Matthew 19:21). This rich man was not told to do the same as rich Zaccheus. The reason is that His New Testament was not in force and would not be until His death, so He could change the requirements of salvation under different conditions.

The sinful woman in Luke 7:50 was told, "Thy faith hath saved thee."

These are examples of salvation but they are not examples we are to follow for salvation, for they took place under a different law and period of time. Examples for us are under the New Testament.

After the Cross A page of history was turned on the Pentecost of Acts 2, when the apostles began to execute the last will and testament of our Lord and Saviour Jesus Christ. They announced the conditions of salvation for the first time. These who met the terms of salvation were saved and added to the church. The pattern for salvation was set that day and all others who have been saved since that time, have done the same things and for the same reasons.

The pattern for salvation is so simple that the masses of people are missing it. On being taught about the death, burial, and resurrection of Christ, the people were fully convinced that Jesus Christ is the Son of God. Peter's sermon was designed to do that very thing. The people were pricked in their hearts, which means they believed Peter's preaching.

This very important question came to the apostles: "Men and brethren, what shall we do?" They not only believed Jesus is the Son of God, they now understand they are sinners and want to know what to do to be forgiven. The answer is clear, inspired, and powerful. "Then Peter said unto them, Repent, and be baptized every one of you in the name of Jesus Christ for the remission of sins, and ye shall receive the gift of the Holy Ghost" (Acts 2:38).

These believers in Christ are told to do two things: repent AND be baptized. The conjunction "and" ties together repentance and baptism and they are done for the same purpose. One does not repent in order to have remission of sins, and be baptized because one is already saved. Whatever one is for, the other one is for.

THREE ANSWERS TO THE SAME QUESTION

In Acts 16:30, the jailer asked, "What must I do to be saved?" He was told to believe. In Acts 2:37, the same question is asked but they are told to repent and be baptized. In Acts 22:10, Saul asked the same question and was told to be baptized. These are three different answers to the same question. Does that surprise you?

Suppose you had never been to the capital city, so you stop to ask directions. You ask how far is it to the capital and they reply thirty miles straight ahead. After going a ways you stop and ask how far to the capital and they reply twenty miles straight ahead. Again, you stop and ask the same question and the reply is ten miles straight ahead. Does that bother you that you got three different answers to the same question? Would you think the people were crazy or playing a trick on you? No, for you received different answers because you were not standing at the same place when you asked the question.

In the same way, the jailer, the 3,000, and Saul were not standing at the same place spiritually when they asked the question. The first thing a heathen jailer should be told to do is to believe. No need to talk to him about baptism. He needs to believe. The 3,000 were believers, so they were told to repent and be baptized. No need to tell them to believe. Saul was a believer and his actions show he had repented, so he was told to be baptized. The different answers make good sense because some of them had already met some of the conditions of salvation.

One must make a personal application to his life by examining what he has done and where he stands, and complete his obedience to God.

QUESTIONS

1. Discuss original sin and why sin cannot be inherited.

2. Distinguish between consequences and guilt of sin.

3. In what sense do we now have eternal life?

4. Name and discuss God's part in our salvation.

5. Name and discuss man's part in his own salvation.

6. Discuss the examples of salvation before the cross and why they are not examples of salvation for us.

7. Consider three answers to the same question.

11 THE MISSION WE HAVE

The greatest problem we face In the church is the danger of putting second things first. This happens also in families. Often parents look out for the physical, educational, and health of their children but give little time or effort in helping them develop spiritually. It is not bad to help them in these areas but the most important thing is their relationship to God and should be the number one concern.

College students sometimes spend so much time in social and fun activities that they neglect the main reason for being in college. We need to learn what is important and decide what should be first.

When Charles M. Schwab was president of Bethlehem Steel, he asked Ivy Lee, a management consultant, to show him a way to get more work done. Lee told him to write down the things he wanted done and number them according to their importance. The next day start on number one and finish it before going to number two. Continue on the list in this way. If the list is not completed, he could be assured that more work was done and that the most important things were done. In a few weeks Charles Schwab sent Ivy Lee a check for $25,000 for the idea.

WHAT WAS THE MISSION OF CHRIST?

The mission of the Church is the same as the mission of Christ. Let us hear Jesus tell us why He came.

"For the Son of man is come to seek and to save that which was lost" (Luke 19:10). "The thief cometh not, but for to steal, and to kill, and to destroy: I am come that they might have life, and that they might have it more abundantly" (John 10:10). He came to fulfill the scripture (Luke 4:17- 21). When Pilate asked Jesus if He is a king, Jesus replied: "To this end was I born, and for this cause came I into the world, that I should bear witness unto the truth" (John 18:37).

It is true that Jesus worked many types of miracles, some of which had compassion as their basis but the basic purpose of His works was to get people to believe. "But these are written, that ye might believe that Jesus is the Christ, the Son of God; and that believing ye might have life through his name' (John 20:31).

When Jesus fed five thousand, He knew that after having been with Him for a long time, they would faint if they had to leave without food. The element of compassion was certainly present but the main reason was to show them He is the bread of life (John 6:35).

When the palsied man was brought to Jesus, He said, "son thy sins be forgiven thee" (Mark 2). He healed the man but it was to show them He could forgive sins. He came to save, to give abundant life, and to deliver people from the bondage of sin.

WHAT IS THE MISSION OF THE CHURCH?

Just as the mission of Christ was to seek and save the lost, so the mission of the church is to preach the gospel to every creature for the same reason.

Greater Works "Verily, verily, I say unto you, He that believeth on me, the works that I do shall he do also; and greater works than these shall he do; because I go unto my Father" (John 14:12).

Jesus says His disciples will do greater works than He did. But what does that mean? he surely does not mean they will do greater miracles than He did, for He did what no one else could do (Matthew 17:16).

The word "works" is not in the Greek text and the King James translators put it in italics, which means they supplied that word. Other translations say greater "things" than these shall they do.

When our Lord began His earthly work after He was baptized by John in the Jordan river, He went from village to village preaching the kingdom (Luke 4:43). For about three and one-half years He taught the people, performed miracles, and gave His parables. At times many followed Him but His popularity declined and as a whole the people rejected Him.

But the apostles and faithful preachers have been able to do greater works than He did while here. Even on the first day, the church had about three thousand converts because of gospel preaching. That number increased to five thousand men in a short time. From Jerusalem and Judea, the gospel went to Samaria, and then to the entire world. In about thirty years the apostle Paul could write that the gospel has been preached to every creature (Colossians 1:23).

The great work of preaching and teaching the gospel which is so powerful it saves sinners and changes lives, must be the "greater works" which Jesus refers to that will be done by believers. He assigned gospel preaching to men "because I go to the Father."

HOW ARE WE DOING ON THIS DIVINE MISSION?

World Population is Exploding In 1850 world population was one billion. In 1930 it had grown to two billion. In 1960 it was three billion. On March 28, 1976 we had four billion, and on July 7, 1986 we reached five billion.

Some unknown author wrote: "If all the unsaved people in the world were to line up single file at your door, the line would reach around the world 30 times. This line would grow by 20 miles each day. If you were to drive 50 miles an hour for 10 hours each day, it would take you 4 years and 40 days to get to the end of the line of lost souls; and, by then, it would have grown by 30,000 more miles."

What is the present condition?

1. The world is lost (2 Corinthians 4:3-4)

2. Number of missionaries has declined, though recently this number has begun to increase.

3. Number of men preparing to preach has dropped drastically.

4. Young couples are willing to go but have no support.

5. Emphasis in our congregations is not on evangelism but on buildings, parking lots, carpet, and other material things.

6. Many congregations have turned inward to teach themselves in one workshop after another.

It is Easy to Get Side-Tracked Have you noticed a train on a side-track? It goes no where. It is not on the mainline. When we get side-tracked from our main reason for existence, we often turn to recreation or social issues, but mostly we turn inward. Instead of teaching others, we teach ourselves.

Satan is not afraid of a busy church unless it is a soul winning church. He does not care how busy we get doing "church work" as long as we are not winning souls.

<u>Why Aren't We Getting the Job Done?</u> It is not because we don't know our mission. Most members of the church can quote the Great Commission, so we do know our mission.

It is not because we don't have the money. Members of the church have good jobs and are highly educated. We make more money than we have ever made, and fortunately, many have been well taught on stewardship and give liberally of their money.

It is not because of a lack of training. Most congregation have men who can preach when asked to do so.

It is not because of a lack of aids. We have filmstrips, charts, books, tracts, and projectors. If anything else can be found that will be helpful, we will buy it too.

It is not because we are too small to do the work. Jesus started with twelve men and told them to take the gospel to the world. Congregations have grown over the past few years, some to become very large. We are large enough to do the work the Lord expects us to do.

The Lord will provide all the money, opportunities, and people to do all He expects us to do. It is His work and He will open doors and help us to do the work. His mission has not changed. He still wants all men to come to a knowledge of the truth (1 Timothy 2:4). He still wants all men to come to repentance (2 Peter 3:9). In order to get His work done, He has put the gospel in the hands of men (2 Corinthians 4:7).

It is the Lord's plan that men tell other men how to be saved. When Saul asked the Lord what he must do, Jesus did not answer him but told him to go into the city and someone would tell him (Acts 9:6). Ananias was directed to tell him what to do. Surely, Jesus knew what Saul needed to do, for He was the Saviour!

Though Cornelius saw an angel and had a vision, he did not learn what to do to be saved that way. It was only after Peter came to him that he learned the way of salvation.

Jesus had told the apostles to go preach the gospel to every creature, and when He was asked what to do, He refused to take from men the responsibility He had given them. It is still true that it pleases God to save people through gospel preaching (1 Corinthians 1:21).

Conclusion

This chapter is not meant to be negative, for we are making some progress but the job is not complete. Many congregations are working almost to the capacity of their money, talent, and leadership. These are to be commended, for it is because of brethren like this that we have made such progress. Some churches are training members to be effective in teaching and evangelism.

But brotherhood-wide we are not doing it. The first step to improve is to know where we stand, so we can recognize where we need to improve. When we point out our weaknesses or failures, it is simply to draw attention to areas we need to strengthen.

A Story   The story is told that after Jesus had suffered the pain, agony, and disgrace of the cross that on His return to heaven the angels gathered around Him to discuss His mission to the earth. One angel said, "It must have been a horrible and dark day when you died for sinners. What plan do you have to see that every person hears about what was done on the cross?" Jesus said, "I selected twelve men to go preach the gospel to every creature; those who believed and were baptized were then to teach others what they have learned and obeyed." Another angel said, "Master, suppose those twelve men fail to do it; and suppose those they baptize neglect, get tired or lazy, and do not preach the gospel, what other plan do you have?" He replied, "I have no other plan."

QUESTIONS

1. What was the mission of Christ?

2. What is the mission of the church?

3. Discuss the meaning of John 14:12

4. What is the world population?

5. What is the present status of world evangelism and why are we not getting the job done?

6. Relate the story of Jesus' return to heaven.

12 THE DAY WE WORSHIP

The day observed under the law was the seventh day sabbath. "But the seventh day is the sabbath of the Lord thy God" (Deuteronomy 5:14). The sabbath was never the first day, and the first day, Sunday, was never Saturday, the seventh day. So, why do we worship on the first day? Is there any scriptural basis for it?

OLD TESTAMENT LAW ABOLISHED

If one is to understand his duty to God today, there must be the recognition and a clear understanding that the Bible contains two testaments and both of them cannot be in force at the same time.

Hebrews 10:9 "He taketh away the first, that he may establish the second." Can one misunderstand such a simple statement? The first, or Old Testament, was taken away. That would mean any law they had has been removed and is not binding on us. The law was nailed to the cross (Colossians 2: 14)

Does that mean we can steal, kill, commit adultery, and covet without sin now? Of course, those things are sin, but not because they are stated in the Old Testament but because they are condemned in the New Testament.

Hebrews 9:16-17 "For where a testament is, there must also of necessity be the death of the testator. For a testament is of force after men are dead; otherwise it is of no strength at all while the testator liveth."

The Holy Spirit illustrates this great truth under the figure of a will. Some time ago we made a new will because we had changed states and needed to update our will. The first thing we did was to look at the old will and see what part of it we wanted to include in the new one. Some new things were added and changes made.

When God made the second will, He included some things that were in the old one and added some things not in the first one. There is no command we obey because it was commanded in the Old Testament. If we were to take part of the Old Testament, we would be obligated to take all of it (Galatians 5:3). We are saved by the New Testament and from it gain authority for what we do.

Much of the Old Testament is history, and history cannot be obeyed. Genesis 1:1 says God created the heaven and the earth. This is history. Moses revealed the divine account of the beginning of things. We don't obey history but we learn from it. Further more, history was not removed at the cross. Genesis 1:1 is just as true now as it was when Moses wrote it. History may affect what you believe and what you do, but you cannot obey it. What we do obey are laws or command, and these Old Testament laws were taken away at the cross.

The Old Testament has great value to the Christian. The "things written aforetime were written for our learning" (Romans 15:4). It reveals the origin of things and is an inspired historical record. Without a study of the Old Testament we could not understand many New Testament passages. It is a book of examples from which we can learn that God blesses the faithful and punishes the disobedient. It reveals the nature of God and the nature of man. But we are not under the laws of the Old Testament.

Galatians 3:24-25 "Wherefore the law was our schoolmaster to bring us unto Christ, that we might be justified by faith. But after that faith is come, we are no longer under a schoolmaster." This is pure logic. 1) The law was our schoolmaster 2) We are no longer under the schoolmaster 3) Therefore, we are no longer under the law.

Ephesians 2:14-15 "For he is our peace, who hath made both one, and hath broken down the middle wall of partition between us; having abolished in his flesh the enmity, even the law of commandments contained in ordinances; for to make in himself of twain one new man, so making peace."

The law was the middle wall that separated Jews and Gentiles, which Jesus broke down and removed. This places both of them on the same basis before God. Paul tells what the mystery is, which had not been revealed in other ages. "That the Gentiles should be fellow heirs, and of the same body, and partakers of his promise in Christ by the gospel" (Ephesians 3:6).

WE ARE UNDER LAW

Though we are not under the Old Testament law, this does not mean we are under no law at all. If there is no law, there would be no sin and no standard of right and wrong. There could be no false teachers.

JAMES 1:25 "But who looketh in the perfect law of liberty, and continueth therein, he being not a forgetful hearer, but a doer of the work, this man shall be blessed in his deed."

ROMANS 8:2 "For the law of the Spirit of life in Christ Jesus hath made me free from the law of sin and death."

GALATIANS 6:2 "Bear ye one another's burdens, and so fulfill the law of Christ."

From these verses we learn we are under the perfect law, the law of the Spirit, and the law of Christ. It is not the law of Moses but it is law. The Spirit gave it but it is law. Christ is the author of it but it is law.

WHAT ABOUT THE FIRST DAY?

From the above passages we have learned that the Old Testament law, including the sabbath, was removed at the cross. The fourth command is not a requirement for us to keep the Sabbath holy. Why, then, do we worship on the first day? Does the Bible say anything about the first day worship?

Psalm 118:22-24 "The stone which the builders refused is become the head stone of the corner. This is the Lord's doing; it is marvelous in our eyes. This is the day which the Lord hath made; we will rejoice and be glad in it."

We must notice each verse carefully. Peter quotes verse twenty-two in Acts 4:11, and makes a direct application to Jesus. In Mark 12:10, Jesus gave the parable of the Wicked Husbandmen, and quotes David's statement and applies it to Himself. From this we understand David refers to Christ.

There is a tradition that when the temple was built that a stone was brought to the site and the builders rejected it and cast it away. Later, they were forced to recover it and found it to be the true corner stone. I don't know if that story is true or not, but this is exactly what happened to Jesus. The spiritual leaders said He did not belong in the building but actually He is the chief corner stone, without which there can be no building.

Verse 23 says, "This is the Lord's doing." This is. What is? Jesus becoming the head stone of the corner is the Lord's doing.

Verse 24 says, "This is the day." What is the day? The day Jesus became the head stone of the corner. "This is the day the Lord hath made." It is the Lord's day. Which day is that? The Lord's day is the day Jesus became the head stone of the corner. He became the head stone of the corner the day He was raised from the dead.

<u>When Was Jesus Raised?</u> Joseph of Arimathea got the body of Jesus on Friday afternoon because it was the day before the sabbath (Luke 23:54). That was after 3:00 p.m. because there was darkness from noon until three (Mark 15:33). Very early the first day He was raised (John 24:1). That "same day" (the first day), Jesus met the two disciples going to Emmaus, and they told Him "today is the third day" (Luke 24:13, 21).

The resurrection day is the first day of the week, and it is the day Jesus became the head stone of the corner. This is the day (resurrection day) that is the Lord's day.

All days belong to the Lord in one sense but the first day is His day because He was raised on that day. Since Pentecost always came on the first day of the week, we know the church began on this day and the apostles began to preach the gospel on that day. We are to eat the Lord's Supper on the first day (Acts 20:7). We are to give of our income on the first day (1 Corinthians 16:1-2).

When John said, "I was in the Spirit on the Lord's day" (Revelation 1:10), we understand him to refer to the first day of the week for "this is the day the Lord hath made; we will rejoice and be glad in it."

We worship on the first day of the week because we have David's prophecy about the Lord's day, and the sabbath was a part of the law that was abolished at the cross. We have both command and example for worship on the first day of the week, which is Sunday.

QUESTIONS

1. Read Deuteronomy 5:14.

2. Study verses that teach the law ended at the cross.

3. Are we under law under the Christian age?

4. Study Psalm 118:22—24.

5. When was Jesus raised?

6. What day is called the Lord's day?

ALBERT GARDNER

13 THE WORSHIP ON THAT DAY

In the last chapter we concluded we are to worship on the first day of the week. Now, we consider the worship on that day. What is acceptable worship? What are we to do? Does the New Testament furnish any information about worship, or are we left on our own judgment and desires?

WHAT IS WORSHIP?

It has been said that everything we do is worship, but this fails to correctly distinguish between worship and service. It is true that our service to God must come from a heart filled with love and a sense of humility, but service is not worship.

When Satan offered Him all the kingdoms of the world, Jesus replied by quoting Deuteronomy 6:13. "Thou shalt worship the Lord thy God, and him only shalt thou serve" (Matthew 4:10). Worship is one thing and service is something else.

Abraham was told to offer Isaac as a sacrifice on mount Moriah. When they got to the place, "Abraham said to his young men, abide ye here with the ass; and I and the lad will go yonder and worship, and come again to you" (Genesis 22:5). What Abraham had been doing was not worship. He said he would "go yonder and worship."

The wise men asked, "Where is he that is born king of the Jews? for we have seen his star in the east, and are come to worship him" (Matthew 2:2). They had come to worship, which means they had been doing something besides worship. The footnote on verse 2 (ASV) says, "The Greek word denotes an act of reverence whether paid to a creature or to the Creator." Worship is an act.

Three Periods of History

Cain and Abel lived under the first period of Bible history called the Patriarchal Age where God dealt with the father for worship and instruction. The second period, the Mosical Age of about 1500 years, began with Moses, and ended at the cross of Christ. We live under the Christian Age where every Christian is regarded as a priest (1 Peter 2:5). This period began on Pentecost and will continue till the end of time.

Under every period of time God has directed people in matters of worship, but the instructions were not the same for every age. Under Moses, the Jews had an elaborate system which included offering animal sacrifices, burning Incense, and the keeping of certain days. Because we recognize and apply the distinction in the periods of history, we do not offer animals as they did in the past because this is not part of the Instructions God has given us.

Law Abolished

The Old Testament law was nailed to the cross. "Blotting out the handwriting of ordinances that was against us, which was contrary to us, and took it out of the way, nailing it to his cross" (Colossians 2:14). This means as a law it is not binding on us, so we do not go to the Old Testament to learn how we are to worship. We can learn from the examples and history of the Old Testament but we are not bound by the laws of that period.

Since we are not bound by the Ten Commandments, one may wonder if it is permissible to kill, covet, and commit adultery. No, these things were forbidden under the law of Moses, but they are also forbidden in the New Testament. We refrain from doing these things, not because they are forbidden by the Old Testament, but because they are forbidden by the New Testament under which we live.

Worship Today

Jesus did not come to command people to worship, for they already did this. He came to set people right in their worship.

The New Testament refers to four types of worship. There is ignorant worship (Acts 17:23), vain worship (Matthew 15:9), will worship (Colossians 2:23), and true worship. When Jesus talked with the woman at the well, He referred to true worship and gave the ingredients of it.

"But the hour cometh, and now is, when the true worshippers shall worship the Father in spirit and in truth: for the Father seeketh such to worship him. God is a Spirit: and they that worship him must worship him in spirit and in truth" (John 4:23-24).

What is True Worship

True Worship Is Directed To God   One could worship idols but it would not be true worship. Only worship that has God as its object can be called true worship.

True Worship Is In The Right Spirit   This requires reverence, submission, and obedience from a loving heart.

True worship has a certain attitude, without which no one can please God. Cain did not offer to an idol but to the true God, however, his sacrifice was not accepted because back of his offering was the unholy attitude that allowed him to substitute his own way for God's way.

When David was praying about his own sins, he tells the kind of spirit needed in true worship. "The sacrifices of God are a broken spirit: a broken and a contrite heart, 0 God, thou wilt not despise" (Psalm 51:17). That is part of the meaning of "blessed are they that mourn" (Matthew 5:4).

People who grieve about their sins are in the right frame of mind to worship.

True Worship Is In Truth Jesus said the word of God is truth (John 17:17). That means true worship must be according to the word of God. It is the guide and pattern for worship. We are to do only that which the New Testament authorizes us to do, in the way God said do it, and for the purposes He said do it.

It is easy to develop the attitude expressed by Naaman when Elisha did not come out to pray and wave his hands over him. He said, "Behold, I thought" (2 Kings 5:11). Our way is not the best way, but God's way is always right. The word of God does not leave us in the dark about what, when, and how we are to worship.

Acts of True Worship

We are discussing true worship which has God as it object, and is offered in the right spirit and is according to the truth. The New Testament, by command and example, designates certain acts of worship. If we offer true worship, we will give careful attention to these matters.

1. **Singing** We praise God with the fruit of our lips.

"Speaking to yourselves in psalms and hymns and spiritual songs, singing and making melody in your heart to the Lord" (Ephesians 5:19).

"Let the word of Christ dwell in you richly in all wisdom; teaching and admonishing one another in psalms and hymns and spiritual songs, singing with grace in your hearts to the Lord" (Colossians 3:16).

In Colossians 3:16 we are told of some very important things that happen when we sing, which could not happen any other way.

A. <u>We teach</u> Others. Self. When we sing of the power of God, the great love and sacrifice of Jesus, and encourage others with songs of praise, we are teaching them. Unless we are hypocritical we will take to heart the very things we are teaching others. This should be true whether we do it by word or song (Romans 2:21).

B. <u>We admonish</u> By our singing to each other we warn of the dangers and pitfalls that defeat us. We teach and admonish with words. By singing words we teach and admonish others, and at the same time their singing admonishes and teaches us.

Since we teach in song, we must sing the truth. It is no more acceptable to sing error as it is to preach error. Even the kinds of songs are important. There is a place for patriotic songs but not in worship. There are some great songs, such as love songs, which are classic and are sung often but their place is not in the worship.

We are to sing psalms, hymns, and spiritual songs.

C. <u>We sing</u> In doing so we obey God for that is exactly what He told us to do. Everyone agrees that we are to sing. It is the safe ground. We teach, admonish, and sing, none of which can be done with instruments introduced by men. Singing is a time for teaching, rededication, and revival of spirit.

2. **Prayer** It is the heart's desire expressed (Romans 10:1). It is not just a psychological exercise that will make you feel better, but is a sincere communication with God, who loves, cares, and answers.

He does not always answer yes, though He does often give us what we ask for. He may say no, wait, or give us something different and better for us.

There are different types of prayers. "I exhort therefore, that, first of all, supplications, prayers, intercessions, and giving of thanks, be made for all men" (1 Timothy 2:1). Most of the time we offer general prayers which may include something from each of these types of prayers.

3. **Giving** In Acts 4 and 5, early Christians sold houses and lands and gave it to help those in need. The permanent way to finance the church was that each person would give of his income each first day of the week in proportion to his income. Paul had given these instructions to the Galatians, and now teaches the Corinthians the same thing, for this was the universal permanent way funds were to be received (1 Corinthians 16:1-2).

The amount we give is important but so is the spirit in which we do it. "Every man according as he purposeth in his heart, so let him give; not grudgingly, or of necessity: for God loveth a cheerful giver" (2 Corinthians 9:7). Great churches have great givers.

4. **Lord's Supper** The true meaning of the Lord's Supper had been lost at Corinth, so the apostle Paul takes them back to the beginning when Jesus gave it (1 Corinthians 11:23-30). He recalls for them, that Jesus took bread and the fruit of the vine and gave thanks for them and said "do this in remembrance of me."

Such common elements were used to help us remember the greatest event in history! When we eat, we are to examine ourselves to make sure we have not treated something sacred like it is common.

5. **Preaching** At Troas, the church came together to eat the Lord's Supper and Paul preached to them (Acts 20:7). By its very nature the church is a teaching institution. The Great Commission gives the duty to teach every creature in all nations, as well as teaching the new Christians to observe all things. The body is to edify itself (Ephesians 4:16).

Gospel preaching is essential to the growth and development of the church. It pleases God to save those who believe gospel preaching (1 Corinthians 1:21). Strong churches are built by strong faithful preaching. Weak preaching can never built strong churches. A church can never rise above its teaching.

Churches ought to find faithful men who are capable of preaching, and encourage, support, and train them to do this divine work. Small churches can do some of their best work in this way. Some churches have had full time preachers for many years, but they have never produced a preacher from their membership.

UNTRUE WORSHIP

Ignorant Worship "For as I passed by, and beheld your devotions, I found an altar with this inscription, TO THE UNKNOWN GOD. Whom therefore ye ignorantly worship, him declare I unto you." (Acts 17:23).

Have you ever heard someone say "I don't believe in organized religion, I would rather just be spiritual."? Or, have you heard, "I believe all religions are right, after all, we are all working to get to the same place."? Make no mistake, these people speak out of ignorance. They do not understand God as he has revealed himself to mankind. And, it is their willingness to accept their own ignorance that will condemn them.

Vain Worship "But in vain they do worship me, teaching for doctrines the commandments of men." (Matthew 15:9). Vain worship is the most prevalent worship today. Just look at how many denominations exist today. Each has their own creeds, policies, authorities and personalities. Matthew is telling us that those who worship in accordance principles that are not in the Bible are worshiping in vain. Their worship serves only the devil.

Instrumental Music One example of vain worship is in the use of instrumental music in worship. This only applies to worship and not what may be done in the home or school. There is nothing wrong with instruments of music outside of worship. As an art, music produced by instruments is beautiful. The skill and talent of those who play are admired, and the discipline required is recognized and appreciated. What one has the talent to do does not justify it being included in worship.

Some have used the following arguments in an attempt to justify their use of instrumental music in worship. However, I have never heard the one argument that matters. No one has ever argued that they use instruments of music because they believe God prefers it and that He wants it.

1) **David Did It**

We have noted that we do no live under the Old Testament period under which David lived. He certainly did use harps, trumpets, and danced (Psalm 150). David is not our pattern with his several wives and rituals of the law.

2) **No Verse Forbids It**

This is the view that what the word of God does not specifically forbid is permissible. One can readily see some serious problems with this view. Where does the New Testament forbid burning incense, counting beads, instrumental music, rice and meat on the Lord's table, polygamy, or sprinkling?

The silence of the scriptures must be respected. "For it is evident that our Lord sprang out of Judah; of which tribe Moses spake nothing concerning priesthood (Hebrews 7:14). Moses did not need to say there are no priests from Judah, but stated priests are from Levi. He said nothing about Judah. We learn from his silence.

Moses had instructed the priests to take fire from a certain place (Leviticus 16:12), but Nadab and Abihu got fire from a different place "and offered strange fire before the Lord, which he commanded them not" (Leviticus 10:1). God had said nothing about the source of their fire, but they were destroyed because they did not respect His silence.

In Numbers 20:8 Noses was told to "speak to the rock" in order to provide water for the children of Israel. What he did was to strike the rock twice. God did not say "don't strike the rock" for He was silent on that point. Because of this disobedience Moses was not permitted to lead the people into Caanan. In telling Moses what to do He had excluded other things but Moses did not respect the silence of God.

3) **It is an Aid**

Some things do aid us in worship, such as song books, lights, or plates and cups for the Lord's Supper. An aid must not change the command or it becomes an addition instead of an aid. Song books only help us to sing. Cups help us to eat the Lord's Supper. But playing an instrument is a different kind of music and is an addition to the command to sing. It is called an accompaniment but more often than not it is the singer that is accompanying the instruments. The singing stops being worship and becomes entertainment.

4) **It is Included in the Greek Word "PSALLO"**

The instrument is named in Ephesians 5:19. "Speaking to yourselves in psalms and hymns and spiritual songs, singing and making melody in your heart to the Lord." According to the verse, the heart is the instrument that is being spoken of.

If piano, organ, or other instruments are in the Greek word, it would not be possible to worship without those instruments, for God's commands are not optional. However, even those who use instruments agree that it is permissible not to use them, and that they do not always use them. If there is authority for their use, they become a part of the command and must be used.

Conclusion to Instrumental Music

We teach, admonish, and sing, none of which can be done with instruments introduced by men. Neither of these things can be done with a mechanical instrument. One might enjoy what is played and admire the skill of the one playing, but one would not be edified.

Instruments of music in the worship are of recent origin in that they were not taught by Jesus or His apostles, and the church for about six centuries did not use them. Their introduction into worship is a source of division, heartache, and broken fellowship and friendship.

We are told to sing and there is no need to have a command not to play. When we are told what to do it excludes everything else. When the doctor gives a prescription, he tells the kind of medicine we are to get and does not list all the medicines we are not to have. When we go to the restaurant and give our order, the waitress does not need to write down all the foods we don't want. When she writes down what we want, she excludes all else.

In the same way, God said sing. There is no need for a command not to play.

Other Examples of Vain Worship

Although musical instruments are probably the most common source of vain worship, there are others. There are those who ignore the example provided by the scriptures that the met on the first day of the week, Sunday, to take the simple spiritual meal called the Lord's Supper. (Acts 20:7) The vain worshiper tells his followers that he knows better than God and only takes it on occasion as they dictate to themselves. Are they not cautioned by the rebuke Paul gave the Corinthians where they had changed the spiritual meal into a common fellowship meal (1 Corinthians 11:20-29).

Still others have installed choirs, added choreography or otherwise turned the worship into a stage show. And finally, ignoring the direct prohibition of the scriptures those that worship in vain have promoted women to positions of leadership even to installing them in the pulpit. This is not a matter of opinion, to have a woman speak in the worship assembly is to deny that the scriptures are inspired by God. (2 Timothy 3:16-17).

"Let your women keep silence in the churches: for it is not permitted unto them to speak; but they are commanded to be under obedience, as also saith the law. And if they will learn any thing, let them ask their husbands at home: for it is a shame for women to speak in the church." (1 Corinthians 14:34-35)

WILL WORSHIP "Which things have indeed a shew of wisdom in will worship, and humility, and neglecting of the body; not in any honour to the satisfying to the flesh." (Colossians 2:23). Will worship was part of the Colossian Heresy, which included parts of the old law, speculation, worshiping angels and making laws about "touch not, taste not, handle not." Their worship was of their own will.

THERE IS NO PATTERN FOR WORSHIP

It is hard to believe that anyone would be serious in offering this as a defense for any change they have made for worship, for if there is no pattern anything would be acceptable. One could worship any thing and any way of his own choosing. The chaos would be unacceptable to God or man.

WE DON'T NEED AUTHORITY FOR WORSHIP

It is equally as hard to believe anyone who believes the Bible would make such a claim. From beginning to end, the authority of God is at stake in our obedience. If no authority is needed, we become a law unto ourselves.

Need for the Assembly

The sabbath was a day of rest. Though we don't have the same restrictions of the law, the Lord's Day has an element of rest. Worship will revive the spirit and strengthen us for daily struggles in our spiritual warfare. How we worship is important, just as important is the assemble itself.

It often happens that when people most need the strength they can get through worship, fellowship, and teaching, they drop out and fail to assemble with fellow Christians (Hebrews 10:25).

QUESTIONS

1. What are three elements of true worship?

2. What is worship?

3. Discuss three things we do in Colossians 3:16.

4. Study one by one the acts of worship.

ABOUT THE AUTHOR

Albert Gardner: Began preaching at age nineteen. He married Frances Eades in 1948. They have five children and twelve grandchildren. Albert and Frances served as missionaries for four years to Ghana West Africa. He has made twenty mission trips to India since 1974. Frances has made about half that many trips to teach the women. The major part of his work in recent times is writing books for India. He has seventeen books that have been translated and printed in Telegu.